WHY I STILL CARRY A GUITAR

Published by **MOTIVATE PUBLISHING**

DUBAI: Media One Tower, Dubai Media City
PO Box 2331, Dubai, UAE
Tel: (+971 4) 4273000, Fax: (+971 4) 428 2268
e-mail: books@motivate.ae
www.booksarabia.com

ABU DHABI: Sheikh Omar bin Zayed Tower, Street No. 9
PO Box 43072, Abu Dhabi, UAE
Tel: (+971 2) 677 2005, Fax: (+971 2) 677 0124

LONDON: Acre House, 11/15 William Road, London NW1 3ER
e-mail: motivateuk@motivate.ae

DIRECTORS: Obaid Humaid Al Tayer, Ian Fairservice
GENERAL MANAGER BOOKS: John Deykin
SENIOR EDITOR: Poonam Ganglani
ASSISTANT EDITOR: Scott Hamilton
CONSULTING EDITOR: Alexander Zolas
SENIOR ART DIRECTOR: Victor Mingovits
SENIOR PRODUCTION EDITOR (ARABIC): Rehab A. Barham
ARABIC EDITOR: Saba Odeh

© Yusuf Islam, 2014

The views expressed in this book are solely those of the author and do not necessarily reflect the views of the publisher.

All rights reserved. No part of this publication may be reproduced in any material form (including photocopying or storing in any medium by electronic means) without the written permission of the copyright holder. Applications for the copyright holder's written permission to reproduce any part of this publication should be addressed to the publishers. In accordance with the International Copyright Act 1956 and the UAE Federal Copyright Law No. (7) of 2002, Concerning Copyrights and Neighbouring Rights, any person acting in contravention of this copyright will be liable to criminal prosecution and civil claims for damages.

British Library Cataloguing-in-Publication Data.
A catalogue record for this book is available from the British Library.

ISBN: 978 1 86063 392 8

Printed and bound in the UAE by Rashid Printers

WHY I STILL CARRY A GUITAR

THE SPIRITUAL JOURNEY *of* CAT STEVENS *to* YUSUF

YUSUF ISLAM

Reasons · 1

Background · 7

The Qur'an · 13

Shahadah · 19

The Community · 25

The Muslim World · 31

Trouble · 37

The Call · 45

Return to Da'wah through Harmony · 51

Children and Song · 59

A Guitar Comes Home · 65

The New Wave · 73

An Other Cup · 79

My People · 85

God is the Light · 93

Endnotes · 97

Image Credits · 101

Key Terms · 103

REASONS

Once the Last Prophet Muhammad (peace be upon him) was walking with his wife, Safiyyah bint Huyay, when two companions from the Ansar passed by them. The Prophet called them and said, 'She is my wife, Safiyyah bint Huyay.' They were surprised and asked him why he said that. He replied, 'Satan flows inside people like blood, I feared maybe he put bad thoughts in your minds about me.' [1]

There are many negative perceptions that swim around in people's minds because of a lack of knowledge or simply misguided imagination; they are quick to judge others. The Prophet (peace be upon him) explained this as the influence of the enemy of mankind, Satan, whispering into people's hearts and filling them with dark and nasty thoughts.

Admittedly, there have been times when I have done things that looked out of the ordinary and surprised people. I walked away from the music business after all; money, a fast-life, love and fame – you don't find many people doing that without raising a lot of eyebrows!

My abrupt departure from the spotlight confused many of my friends and fans. Sadly, a few decided to believe strange rumours about my decision based on inaccurate information and myths, propagated mostly by the media. This circulated in the vacuum caused by my sudden withdrawal from the music world.

My surprise return to music may again raise many eyebrows and justifiably invite questions from people. While some critics might view it as a step backward, I see my music as a positive continuation of my intention to build roadways to peace, convey a moral message and dispel ignorance. Having made a study of the subject for more than twenty-five years – indicating that I do not take the issue lightly – I am now personally sure of a broader allowance for art and music in Islam. This is because of the fact that there is more evidence indicating allowance, rather than prohibition, based on the Qur'an and *Hadith*,[2] which I will explain in a bit more detail later in this book.[3]

Witnessing the way in which Islam has been misunderstood, as well as the way some Muslims themselves misinterpret and abuse the fundamentals of the religion, has caused me to think and work in different ways. One of the biggest challenges we face, and which is largely left unattended, lies outside the safe protective confines of Muslim schools, institutions and mosques. In the busy commercial streets, in the media and public arenas, Islam's message is obscured or totally misrepresented. Cloaked in mystery and suspicion, Satan has managed to cover the Divine light of truth and happiness and replace it with a terrifying image of fear and hatred.

The great gift of mercy, which the last Prophet personified, has been trampled on and covered with dust and dirt by a new and dangerous revival of pre-Islamic, Makkan-style propaganda associating Muslims with terrorism, lawlessness and endless wars. Unfortunately, the new, well-equipped army of shadows has been assisted by some who carry Muslim names and causes. They never seem to follow or support the Prophet's first and foremost mission: to deliver the clear promise of everlasting prosperity through following God's revelation and to do good works that benefit humanity.

The Prophet Muhammad (peace be upon him) was the last Messenger to be sent for the guidance of all, not just for a section of humanity, and we learn this religion from him. For a newcomer to Islam, it is a process of rediscovering all the great and honourable teachers of mankind such as Jesus, Solomon, David, Moses and Abraham, to mention just a few. Their message has been clarified and restored through the life and teachings of the last Prophet, may the peace and blessings of God be upon them all.

Not a messenger did we send before thee without this inspiration sent by us to him: that there is no god but I; therefore worship and serve Me.[4]

Now, some 1,400 years after the revelation of the Qur'an and Muhammad's passing, (peace be upon him) there are no more prophets to come apart from the prophesied return of Jesus, son of Mary,[5] near the end of the world. As one billion Muslims try to navigate without the existence or institution of a Caliph (successor to the Prophet), it is clear that there are many complications, particularly concerning the interpretation and application of the Qur'an and the Prophet's *Sunnah* (the 'way' of the Prophet, what he practiced) in today's confused and fractured world.

'Make things easy, don't make them difficult; give good news, don't make people run away'[6] the Prophet (peace be upon him) said. But the good news and the instructions of the Prophet have been forgotten and a lot of people are fearful. Today, the call to paradise is drowned out by the hellish noise of war and discord. The declaration of *La ilaha illa-Allah*,[7] the oneness of God and belief in His Messenger, is mostly heard by mourners of the dead in the aftermath of destroyed towns and villages, or during marches and rallies, where Muslims look angry, shaking fists whilst shouting and burning flags or images of Western world leaders.

'My abrupt departure from the spotlight confused many of my friends and fans. Sadly, a few decided to believe strange rumours about my decision based on inaccurate information and myths.'

Regrettably, many Muslims inherited Islam at birth and have not necessarily studied it or acquired the skill of explaining the faith very well. A lot make the mistake of assuming everybody already knows the basics. But very few people – including Muslims themselves – possess the motivation to research the subject properly; some folk don't even have the time to read the instructions on the box of goods or equipment they have just bought from a shop! If a person never gets to know a good practising Muslim, then it is likely that he would be left judging Islam only by the picture provided by the media or a Muslim colleague or neighbour who, because of fear, keeps their faith private in order not to be noticed or targeted by Islamophobes or racists.

Therefore, there are many important reasons for me to return to the public eye. Because of fame and the fact that many people around the world already knew me as Cat Stevens, my embracing Islam became a reference and a story of intrigue for them. Many people naturally want to understand how an iconic, long-haired, hippy pop star that sang and embodied their dreams ended up a Muslim, prostrating in prayer five times a day and abandoning drinks, parties, adoration and applause.

I have been allowed to traverse through many cultural thresholds and seen and done many things. Also, my understanding of Islam has obviously evolved over these past decades. It would certainly be quite unnatural if I had remained at the same level of knowledge that I entered with as a new Muslim in 1977. Change is necessary and undeniable, as the all-Knowing tells us in the pages of the wise book:

You will certainly travel from stage to stage.[8]

As you journey, things you discover often alter or expand your previous views. Regrettably, this is not the case with everybody; many people in the world haven't dared to move very far away from where they began. Most of the earth's inhabitants still haven't stepped out to understand or check out what Islam truly is.

I was blessed with an enquiring mind and a fascination for knowledge about what lies outside the walls we often choose to hide behind. So, here is a short background of the journey I took from *Jahiliyyah*[9] to Islam, and – importantly – why I still carry a guitar.

> Well I left my happy home to see what I could findout
> I left my folk and friends
> With the aim to clear my mind out
> Well, I hit the rowdy road and many kinds I met there
> Many stories told me of the way to get there.[10]

BACKGROUND

I had quite an amazing youth and background. Born in the centre of London's West End, my home stood between the busy red bus routes of Shaftesbury Avenue on one side and New Oxford Street on the other. So my playground was a triangle, somewhere between Piccadilly Circus, Trafalgar Square and the British Museum. That was where my life began.

I received quite a strict Christian upbringing in a Catholic School called St Joseph's, off Drury Lane, in the heartland of clubs, cinemas and theatres. Not surprising, perhaps, that the entertainment world was an obvious option for me. It was the easiest thing in the world to step out of my front door and straight to the stage door of the theatre across the road or Tin Pan Alley, rather than go to church.

As a child I was inspired to be an artist like my uncle Hugo in Sweden, who was a painter. But then gradually I saw that many painters died poor and this society did not give much credence to people who were poor. Everything seemed geared towards material success and becoming a 'winner'. The American image of the 'good life' was projected everywhere. New films and television series were continuously flooding in.

> '*The exquisite goal of the popular American dream was to be on top: get rich, be young and good-looking. I fitted most of those categories when I made it at the grand old age of eighteen.*'

Marilyn Monroe, James Dean, Frank Sinatra and Elvis – these were some of the mass-manufactured icons of Hollywood's dream machine.

My father Stavros came from a small village in Cyprus. He was a smart, hardworking man who had migrated to Egypt then the US for work in the mid-twenties before landing in London. He knew the value of bread and ran the family restaurant. Inheriting his work ethic, at the age of eight I began serving in the shop as a waiter and mopping the floors, to earn a bit of extra pocket money.

The exquisite goal of the popular American dream was to be on top: get rich, be young and good-looking. I fitted most of those categories when I made it at the grand old age of eighteen as a popular songwriter and singer, with the name Cat Stevens.

Music was the fastest way to make a million, The Beatles had proved it, and they inspired me. It wasn't long before I had hit records and was pushed out on the road. However, in that initial twelve-month period of fame and success in 1967, having spent most of my good health on drinking, smoking and late nights, I got struck down with tuberculosis.

Suddenly, finding myself flat on my back in a hospital bed, gazing up at the ceiling with the pop business whizzing past me, I was left to wonder: 'What happened?'

Lying there in hospital, deep in the countryside, surrounded by doctors and nurses, I asked myself a lot of important questions; what if I died – what would happen to me then?

At that time there was a great interest in things Eastern, things transcendental. The Beatles had gone to India and a friend had given me a copy of a Buddhist book called *The Secret Path*. That was the beginning of my search for explanations: for clear, truthful answers about the meaning of existence and where this life could possibly lead to – especially after death. That frightful thought of the unknown began to affect my view of life and the ultimate purpose of being human. I started meditating.

After I came out of my convalescence, after about a year in fact, I had grown a beard and had started writing music again with a new spirit and deeper insight. A lot of my songs were now much more personal and soulful. I didn't want any business managers or record bosses to tell me how to make my music: I wished to be free to express my ideas the way I wanted to hear them, simple and raw.

The new songs I wrote were uncluttered, dominated by a six-string guitar; full of spiritual enquiries, my words exposed an openness and childlike honesty.

> I wish I knew, I wish I knew,
> What makes me, me
> And what makes you, you
> It's just another point of view. [11]

At first there were not many people interested in the new 'folksy' me, but finally I found a new manager, Barry Krost, and he got me a new contract with a forward-looking company called Island Records. Chris Blackwell, the boss of Island Records, was an intuitive man with a love of music.

He was won over by listening to my new song, 'Father & Son'. Blackwell's faith paid off when my second career skyrocketed in a way we could never have dreamed. My albums began selling fast, especially in the United States during a time when there was a strong appetite for a gentle, acoustic and reflective musical style.

Those were the melodious seventies, and my songwriting suddenly blossomed. But throughout the experience one of the most important hallmarks of my songwriting – discernable in my lyrics particularly – was a clear sense of *searching*. I was studying and reading a strange mix of books on Hinduism, Taoism, Zen, vegetarianism and numerology, which, combined with my Christian upbringing, all contributed to the background and metaphors within my songs. Looking back into my albums, a person today would see quite clearly that within me was a fluttering soul that could not settle down; always seeking something supremely higher.

My records were selling in the millions all over the world; people were queuing up to see me live in concert halls and arenas. I had reached the status of 'Superstar'. But even with all the adoration, I was still restless and empty inside, blowing here and there – a snowflake, frightened to land in case I melted before reaching the mountain top.

So I continued on my upward journey to seek the ultimate truth whilst still being surrounded by managers and agents; booked on heavy tours, flying around various countries and towns, spotlighted on stage in front of thousands of loving fans. That balancing act wasn't very easy; something had to happen.

> Miles from nowhere
> Guess I'll take my time, o yeah
> To reach there. [12]

Something did happen; the incident was a major turning point. One day, below the hills of Malibu in Los Angeles – the famous beach strip of land where a community of millionaires live – I was with my manager at the house of my record chief, Jerry Moss, and decided to take a dip in the ocean. Unknown to me, it was a very dangerous time of the day to swim. I didn't realize while looking out from the beach that there was actually nobody else around in the sea that day, nevertheless that was part of my 'don't-you-dare-tell-me-what-to-do' style.

Dashing to put on my trunks, I ran out for a swim. After about a quarter of an hour the water was freezing, I decided that was enough for one afternoon and tried to return to shore. That's when it struck me – perhaps this wasn't such a clever time to go swimming. I felt the powerful Pacific Ocean current steadily rip me away from the shore. My manager stood on the beachfront by the house thinking everything was alright, but he was so far away he could not have heard me nor done anything.

My legs and arms were now aching and getting too weak and limp to swim back to land. This was it. Finally, in that split second, I realized there was no other help and called out, praying from the depths of my sinking heart, 'O God, if You save me, I'll work for You!' At that moment, a gentle wave came from behind me and pushed me forward. Instantly, with all the strength that I needed, I began swimming back to shore and within a few minutes, my feet touched land and I was there, safe and alive. That was my moment of truth!

I always knew that God existed, and on that fateful day I renewed my relationship with Him in the form of a contract out in the ocean. But as usual, what happens with us humans after being saved from the jaws of a storm and the weather settles down, is that we easily forget what we promised and go about our usual business again. But of course, a promise is never forgotten by God and the time was to come when it had to be fulfilled.

> I listen to the Wind
> To the wind of my soul
> Where I end up? Well, I think
> Only God really knows. [13]

THE QUR'AN

The big opportunity came when my elder brother David journeyed to Jerusalem. He had married a Jewish girl from Tel Aviv, and in 1975 he took a trip to the Holy Land to visit her family. It was a miniature pilgrimage for him.

Like my elder sister Anita and me, David was brought up on the Bible as a Christian; he went to the same Roman Catholic school. My brother was a thinker and had a strong feeling of respect and love for the sacred places and roads where Jesus and the prophets had walked and delivered their teachings. But during his visit to Jerusalem he became quite upset by the divisions and bickering he witnessed between some priests from different Christian churches.

One day he gazed across a golden domed mosque that stood at the centre of the Holy City and thought, 'What is this religion?' Islam was relatively unknown in the West and David was a brave enough sort to go and step inside.

He felt a sense of peace, walking shoeless around the mosque and seeing the way that Muslims worshipped: no statues, no pictures, just pure, serene prayer. All this impressed him immensely.

'I saw this golden dome, which was never there before. That was the symbol of everything that I was discovering about Islam: suddenly it was there when it wasn't there before.'

London played host to a low-key festival of Islam in 1976. David saw a translation of the Qur'an in one of the shops and said to himself: 'This is the Holy Bible of the Muslims'. Since he knew that I was a reader of such books he bought it for me as a birthday gift. The book, a beautifully gold-bound publication from Japan, came into my hands as a complete surprise. My brother was not a Muslim but he had been touched by something very spiritual inside the mosque.

Little did I know when setting out on the Secret Path all those years ago what mysteries I would discover. Reading the Qur'an was the beginning of my entrance into God's university of the Divine script. The very first revelation to the Prophet was the perfect embodiment of my own first encounter with the message of Islam:

> **Read in the name of your Lord Who creates,**
> **Creates man from a lowly clot**
> **Read! And your Lord is most Generous,**
> **Who taught by the pen**
> **Taught man that which he knew not.**[14]

It took me about a year to read through the Qur'an, front to back. At the start I had misgivings about Islam; one of the major problems of living in the West. My father was a Greek Cypriot, so that made the image of Muslims even worse for me because of the extreme hatred the Greeks fostered against the Turks. So before reading I consciously tried to remove any prejudice and keep an open mind.

> **In the name of God, the Supremely Merciful, the Most Kind,**
> **All Praise be to God, the Lord of the Worlds.**[15]

Oh, what a welcome surprise it was: The Qur'an was about God – not moons or stars, not strange Arabic idols or deities? It was so unexpected. I was amazed to find that Islam was not that foreign religion which I had imagined; it didn't mention anything about Arab or Turkish nationalism, rather it spoke about the unbreakable link between all mankind as one family, all being the children of Adam. Old images and preconceptions could no longer ambush or attack me from the depths of my own ignorance, now the truth was being exposed – crystal clear.

Firstly, the Qur'an teaches belief in one Supreme Being – the Originator of all creation – referring to humanity as one noble household set on earth as vicegerents to be tried and tested. The verses talk about prophets as brothers preaching the same message of unity, trying to put man back on the track of truth and righteousness. I saw the names of Jesus, Moses, Abraham, Jacob, Noah and, of course, the name of the last Prophet and Messenger of God, Muhammad (peace be upon them).

All the major prophets and messengers are mentioned in the Qur'an, as are the Gospel and the Torah.

It appeared to me that the propaganda invented about the religion of Islam was one of the biggest theological cover-ups in history – or else we all simply had our eyes and ears closed.

> **He (God) has established for you the same religion which He ordained for Noah, and that which We inspire in thee (Muhammad), and that which We commended unto Abraham and Moses and Jesus, saying: be steadfast in the religion, and be not divided therein. Dreadful for the idolaters is that unto which you invite them. Allah chooses for Himself whom He wills, and guides unto Himself those who turn (toward Him).**[16]

When it came to scientific issues the Qur'an seemed to be completely in concurrence with the realities of modern science; mentioning the 'orbiting' of the Sun, Moon and planets; explaining the 'Big Bang'; confirming all living things are made of water, and describing in detail the development of the human foetus within the womb. The verses of the Qur'an were unassailable. I looked for mistakes, but the more I did the more it became clear that the faults were only with me.

> **Can't those who disbelieve see that the heavens and the earth were a joined entity, and We separated them and made from water every living thing? Then will they not believe?**[17]

One of the greatest moments, while I was studying the Qur'an, came while reading the story of Joseph. It's very similar to the version found in the Bible. But towards the end of the chapter, the part that really shook me was when his brothers, who had previously thrown him down the well, were face to face with Joseph. Unaware that he was in front of them, they were talking badly and slandering him. But Joseph kept patient within himself. God! Something resonated inside me, perhaps my own words from the song: 'Father & Son', 'All the times that I've cried, keeping all the things I knew inside'.

That's the point I wept and knew my real identity – I was a Muslim, a surrenderer to God, and the Qur'an was the key to keeping my promise made in the ocean.

The chapter of Joseph is the most beautiful story, as the Qur'an itself says. Reading it opened my heart. I knew then that this book could not have been invented or authored by any human hand. It was truly a revelation. After searching the paths and pages of so many different religions, philosophies and holy books, there was now only one voice that I needed to listen to in this new universe, it was not that of a man, a sage, priest or leader; it was the Word of God. From that moment it became clear there was nothing left for me to do but to surrender and embrace Islam – and that was my next step.

Eventually I found out about a place where I could meet some Muslims. A friend told me that there was now a new mosque in Regent's Park. In fact I'd played and walked in that park so many years of my life, I'd never seen anything there other than mothers and prams, birds, trees and grass. Then suddenly, one day, rising up above the greenery, I saw this golden dome, which was never there before. That was the symbol of everything that I was discovering about Islam: suddenly it was there – when it wasn't there before.

> **Whoever Allah wishes to guide He opens his heart to the surrender (Islam).**[18]

SHAHADAH

One cold wintry Friday in 1977, I took that dramatic step and walked into the London Central Mosque in Regent's Park to declare my belief: 'I testify there is no God but Allah (the one God) and Muhammad is His servant and Messenger' and that's the day I entered the *Ummah* – the nation of faith.

After taking *Shahadah*,[19] I was floating on an invisible cloud of mercy, carrying me upward and away from worldly entanglements. I was still under a contractual obligation to make records, but so many things in the music industry contradicted the Islamic way of life. Even though I was never an excessive, rebellious rock star type, the music world was unfortunately connected to lots of nasty stuff like fornication, idolatry, greed, competition, pride and selfishness – 'Sex, Drugs, Rock & Roll', as it is so often referred to.

The Qur'an didn't specifically mention 'music', but in the back of my mind I realized that, as a new Muslim, it would probably be impossible to accumulate the necessary knowledge and wisdom or to fully practice my faith while still tagging around with the show business circus.

'Even though I was never an excessive, rebellious rock star type, the music world was unfortunately connected to lots of nasty stuff like fornication, idolatry, greed, competition, pride and selfishness – "Sex, Drugs, Rock & Roll".'

In 1978 I released one last album under my Cat Stevens name, put *'Bismillah'* (In the name of Allah) on it and called it *Back to Earth*. I then wrote a polite letter to my record company bosses and asked them to free me from further contractual obligations, saying I wanted a break. They were kind enough to agree. That gave me a lot of time and space to spend, studying and learning how to perfect my prayers and get on with my practice of Islam. I also took the name Yusuf Islam, on 4 July 1978.

> Oh the white boats have landed
> And the innocent are here
> So dream for the child
> Cause it's the time of the year. [20]

I had discovered a new way to view the universe. Like a kid who had travelled by spiritual rocket to an exciting new world, I was weightless, bouncing around, finding my way; learning the streets and the language and making new friends. There was so much to learn. The old haunts and alleyways of my past began to slip away from memory.

Of course, I was very conscious about the importance of this decision. I knew that it would have a big impact on my family, on my friends and on the public. I could imagine what people would say: 'Cat Stevens, the recluse hippy poet, has become a Muslim? You must be joking.' But the most important thing at that moment was not what other people thought – God was my Creator and my Maker, He had saved me and guided me to this, my destiny. There was nothing and no one else I needed to worry about – oh, what bliss!

It was like going back to my pure original nature; back to wide-eyed childhood again. If you really listen to your conscience you will know when something is right. For so long I'd been bullied, forced to conform to other domineering voices telling me to do things, which they and the 'system' expected. I was now truly free from the shackles of superstition and had broken through the narrow prison bars of tradition to a new and uncluttered heavenly horizon.

My family were a little shocked initially, although they had seen me going through fads, trends and fashions before. Maybe they were hoping that it was just a passing phase; but not this time. They knew I was serious. Perhaps it was more difficult for my father because he was from the Greek community, a Cypriot. For the Greeks (as you may know) the historical enemies were the Turks, and the Turks were synonymous with Islam and Muslims.

Thankfully, my father was brought up in Egypt. When he was a young boy he had left Cyprus and had gone to work in Alexandria for some years before setting off on his search for a better life in the US and London. So he was well travelled and obviously knew Islam before I did. In fact, I remember my father always used to say *'Allah Karim, Allah Karim'*

(God is Most Kind). He always showed gratitude to God for blessing our family; we had enough food, we had shelter. So Dad had much in common with Islamic culture and spoke broken Arabic before I did.

I tried to explain Islam to my mother and to my brother and sister. Strangely, the biggest fight I had was with my brother David, who had given me the Qur'an in the first place. Like Joseph, I was now independent and beyond my brother's control. In the end I was able to help my family accept it to one degree or another.

My focus was now turned towards the pleasure of God and the hereafter – at a time when most people around me were looking for material rewards here and now. It was my desire to live a simple Muslim life. So I moved back to North London to be close to my parents; after all, kindness to parents is what Islam teaches and they were getting old. My father was ill, and I dearly wanted him to accept Islam.

One day, while he was in hospital he asked my mother where '*Yusuf*' was, she told him, 'In the mosque.' My father smiled. By the grace of the Almighty, only two days before he died, I was at my father's side and asked him to declare his faith in the one God. Miraculously, in my presence, he spoke the words '*La ilaha illa-Allah*' – and so died a Muslim.

My mother supported me. She was Swedish and had a kind and broad liberal view of life, always smiling. When I started fasting in Ramadan she would help cook the *halal*[21] food and sometimes even fasted with me – may Allah have mercy on both my parents. My mother also made the Testimony of Faith (two years before she passed away) as later did my brother and his son, Daniel. In a way, there was great acceptance in my family once they understood what Islam was all about from the inside rather than the outside.

My friends were perhaps a little bit more difficult because they knew that this spelt the end of my career and in a way I was no longer hooked on the music business. Our points of interest were far apart – for them that changed everything. I suppose that's when I decided there had to be a limit.

The moment came when I was sitting in a restaurant in Soho with some close friends. I had given up drinking. They were indulging in some wine; all of them were getting more and more tipsy. Soon they became mindless and started swearing, raising their glasses saying, 'Hey! Blood of Jesus,' I became upset and said, 'Look! Please, he is our Prophet, you shouldn't...' but before I could go on further, my then close friend, Peter, lunged out and hit me in the face, making my lip bleed. It made it very easy for me after that to know which way to go.[22]

> All the times that I cried
> Keeping all the things I knew inside
> It's hard; but it's harder to ignore it
> If they were right, I'd agree
> But it's them they know not me
> Now there's a way, and I know,
> That I have to go. [23]

THE COMMUNITY

The Central Mosque in London became my gateway into the world community of Muslims, and Muslim organizations and movements. Fortuitously, the mosque had just been built and completed in 1977 – the same year I embraced Islam. On Fridays I would attend the *Jumu'ah* (congregational) prayer and each week I would make more and more acquaintances. Whenever I read the Qur'an there were questions I would ask the chief Imam, the late Dr Syed Mutawalli Ad-Darsh, and he would point me in the right direction.

The new and impressive mosque and towering minaret overlooking Regent's Park was a magnet for Muslims from all over the world. Although it was mostly paid for and financed by the Kingdom of Saudi Arabia, its trustees hailed from almost every Muslim country: Egypt, Libya, Algeria, Indonesia, Malaysia, Sudan, Pakistan, and more. They were ambassadors and diplomats belonging to embassies or consulates based in London.

All that political flower arranging seemed a good thing at the time; it seemed a great image of Muslim unity, lots of lovely colourful flags all together hanging in a line. Being new to Islam, there was much for me to learn.

I was overwhelmed by the feeling of brotherhood and belonging. Whenever a Muslim met me, I felt so at home. Many, when they found out I was a convert (or revert as some exacting people would put it) wanted to hear my story and how I came to Islam. Most had no interest in music and the name Cat Stevens was unknown to them. However, others became highly impressed – 'Did you say Cat Stevens?!' Their embarrassing exclamations echoed round the mosque. But I wanted to remain unrecognized, just an ordinary fellow Muslim – albeit slightly more distinguished by my expensive jeans and shirts than the majority of worshippers.

Some Muslims were quite baffled as to how it was possible for me to grasp the message of Islam simply by reading an English translation of the Qur'an. Frankly, their attitude baffled me much more. I couldn't believe how distant some Muslims had become to the overwhelming magnitude of the Qur'an's message and glaring truth; how numb some were to its incredibly powerful impact. As a similitude, I can only liken it to a group of people who have lived and resided above the clouds on a mountain so long, they became oblivious to it and astonished when a visitor arrives and informs them that they live on a mountain!

Stranger still is the fact that at the point when I decided to embrace Islam, I didn't know a single Muslim. The faith of Islam and Muslims was so well concealed in the West; not many of us were really interested in it, and it was sometimes even confused in my mind with Hinduism and Sikhism (certainly in Britain, Muslims seemed to look, eat and dress the same). The media and history books had omitted any mention of the true universal message of Islam. If anything at all, it was presented instead as a foreign, oriental religion belonging to the dark ages.

In those days the environment in the UK was not entirely hostile to Islam. There was still a general apathy towards the religion, most academics at best saw it as a cultural novelty. 'Orientalism' had made it look like an out-of-date and distant culture, connected to the desert sands, carpets and harems full of beautiful, veiled concubines. The media was relatively quiet on the subject. And to top it all I had to travel miles to find a *halal* meat shop.

'I wanted to remain unrecognized, just an ordinary fellow Muslim.'

Apart from my connection with God through prayer and my newly found family of fellow worshippers at the mosque, the world was distinctly different and I was now feeling a bit lonely. It was time to get married and establish a home.

I was introduced to a good Muslim family through a friend and fellow British Muslim. The head of the family, Mr Mubarak Ali (who looked remarkably like my own Dad, with trimmed moustache and all), had five daughters. After visiting them in their house near Surbiton, I knew pretty soon whom I wanted to marry. When she bashfully accepted, I introduced Fawziah to my mother and after getting her blessing, we married. Ours was the one thousandth marriage at the London Central Mosque and Islamic Cultural Centre, performed by the Chief Imam, Dr Darsh.

Within a year our first daughter was born. We named her Hasanah, which means 'something beautiful and good'. She certainly was – thanks be to God.

It dawned on me that there was a lot of work to be done in the community; what school would I send Hasanah to? One Friday, the director of the mosque gave a powerful speech about the need for Muslim schools: there weren't any established in the UK at that time. I immediately wrote a cheque for forty thousand pounds to the cause. But after a while, the project seemed to die down – great speech, but no follow up.

Along with another four British Muslims, we started a circle for learning Islam at the Central Mosque, trying to convey the message of Islam to visitors. I suppose that's when I first started working for *Da'wah* (calling to Islam) and Islamic education.

The Imam at the centre, Dr Darsh (may Allah grant him mercy) was a wonderful and wise man. He was a true scholar from Al Azhar University, Cairo, and understood the deep cultural problems and issues facing Muslims in the West. In the beginning, when I told him that I was a musician, he did not balk or criticize me, but encouraged me to continue composing and recording. However, he suggested staying away from stage performances. Like most learned scholars, he understood that music was a matter of *Fiqh* (religious understanding), not *Aqidah* (Foundations of Faith); his opinion was that it was allowed within certain moral guidelines.

But I was listening to other voices too. There were some scholars and theologians, particularly those who had studied in Saudi Arabia, who made a strong argument against music, stating that it was *haram* (forbidden). It certainly was a debatable issue as I began considering the contrasting pieces of evidence. I felt uneasy holding a guitar in Muslim company.

Looking back, it's interesting to note now how my formative years as a Muslim were shaped by those I came into contact with. Within a year of embracing Islam, I had visited Makkah and made the *'Umrah* (lesser-pilgrimage). On my way I passed through Egypt and stayed for a few nights in Hassan Square. What amazed me was how the *Adhan*[24] was almost entirely ignored, except for a few dedicated and mostly aged worshippers. Most Muslims seemed not to hear it anymore!

That of course, was not the case in Saudi Arabia, where business stopped, people shut their shops and went to pray when the call to prayer was made. I was deeply impressed.

During that visit, I met a kind Sheikh who invited me home and gifted me with the complete volumes of Sahih Al Bukhari's collection[25] of the Prophet's *Hadith*. He said words to the effect that 'Here is the second most authentic and reliable book to learn and to read after the Qur'an'.

I also visited Madinah where the blessed Prophet (peace be upon him) had migrated and is buried. Coming out of the Prophet's mosque I met

Abu Ameena Bilal Phillips, a Jamaican convert from Canada. He asked me what I did for a living. I told him I was a singer, 'Oh! You'll have to give that up – musical instruments are *haram*.' His bold confidence seemed unquestionable even though, after subsequently scanning through the volumes of *Sahih Al Bukhari*, I did not discover one chapter or clear reference about 'music' in that authentic collection of *Hadith*.

In addition to the criticism of music, back in the 'wild world' I had to deal with the harsh response of the media and journalists' noticeable distaste at my choosing Islam. It was extremely hurtful and derogatory: 'The Cat Sat on the Mat' was the headline on one particularly cynical article, showing an unflattering picture of me gnawing a tomato. The ugly face of prejudice behind the establishment's smiling mask revealed itself – I knew it was best to just get out and enjoy my new life as a Muslim.

By this time I had also had the chance to read some other reference books and discover some sayings of the Prophet about the subject of singing and musical instruments. Although there were positive indications, there were also some negative ones. So one day I decided to remove the lingering doubts and auction my instruments for charity – something I do not regret, except for the confusion and hurt it caused many sincere followers of my life and career. At the time I did not fully appreciate what damage my abrupt departure might have caused to the general image of Islam. But I was in no mood for compromise.

I was now eager to grow my beard as long as possible and – without being conscious of it – quite contrary to the description of the friendly, smiling disposition of the Prophet (peace be upon him), my face began to frown.

As God willed it, I would be given the space and time to learn.

> Oh I'm on my way I know I am
> Somewhere not so far from here
> All I know is all I feel right now
> I feel the power growing in my hair. [26]

THE MUSLIM WORLD

The UK was a melting pot for Muslims from all over the world; many were refugees or migrants seeking a better life and an escape from poverty and tyranny. The Qur'an emphasizes the need for Muslims to be concerned about the poor, and to give generously in charity. The *Zakat* collection boxes in the mosque were therefore always full. Many voices were raised crying against the injustices heaped on oppressed Muslim populations, and there were always pamphlets and leaflets distributed on Fridays calling for support for this or that political cause.

The influence of the *Salafi*[27] movement was growing stronger at the London Central Mosque. They were totally against the idea of music and any form of frivolity or entertainment, considering it and its proceeds *haram*. That argument convinced me to be more cautious. Though I'd stopped making music and had gotten rid of my musical instruments, I became worried about the impact of eating or consuming anything forbidden from money I was still earning from royalties. I dissected my music catalogue and divided it up into *haram*, *makruh* (disliked) and *halal* categories. The *makruh* and *haram* portions I assigned to

> 'Looking at these devoted brothers in white *thawbs*, long dishevelled beards and turbans made me quite envious; they looked like they had just emerged from the dusty sands of time.'

a company with charitable objects, and the *halal* was placed in another publishing company, the income of which, I and my family were able to survive on.

I had also bumped into a group called *Tabligh Jamat* and they had enlisted me to do 'forty days' of travelling and *tabligh* (conveying Islam). During the time I was with them they taught me the basics of Islamic behaviour and etiquette, especially concerning prayer (*Al Salat*) and the importance of punctuality and performing prayer with congregation in the mosque. Since then I have never knowingly missed a prayer all my Muslim life – thanks to God.

Looking at these devoted brothers in white *thawbs*, long dishevelled beards and turbans made me quite envious; they looked like they had just emerged from the dusty sands of time, resembling the *Sahabah* – the close Companions of the Prophet (peace be upon him). A prime goal for me at that time was to try and emulate the *Sunnah*. We regularly read lessons from *Ta'lim ul-Islam*, a book about the stories and lives of the Companions who, through the stories of their immense faith and sacrifice, appeared to take on the characteristics of saints. However, I knew the Qur'an did not promote the concept of 'holy men' and I had often read the principle quoted in Islamic books, repeating: 'there are no priests in Islam'.

The reality is that in God's eternal religion, every believer has a chance to individually approach Him without the need for an intercessor – as the Qur'an says in the first chapter: 'You alone we worship; You alone we ask for help.' Regardless of this unique spiritual leveller – as I was to learn – over the centuries, apart from the illustrious Companions, the Muslim world seemed to have developed a highly evolved hierarchy of distinguished figures and theological branches in the names of early, renowned and pious scholars. I was now asked, 'What *madhhab* (school of thought) do you follow?' Gradually I became introduced to the four major divisions of 'Sunni Islam' [28] next to a fifth, 'Shi'ah Islam'. [29]

At one point a well-meaning brother gave me a book to try and help me learn certain etiquettes – it almost blew me away. There were some one thousand *'masalas'* (questions with juristic answers); one of them stated you had to bury your clipped nails and any cut hair beneath the earth! There were endless dos and don'ts, but none of them gave any reference to the Qur'an or authentic *Hadith*. Being primarily a thinker and a seeker I became fearful of falling into simply an imitational form of Islam (*taqleed*); I was consciously careful not to become an adherent of anyone but the Prophet (peace be upon him). As the Qur'an says:

> **And say (O Prophet): If you love Allah, follow me, Allah will love you and forgive you your sins; verily Allah is forgiving, Most Merciful.** [30]

In no way did I believe the Qur'an required me to attach or extend my faith to anything outside the protection of the preserved words of God or the Prophet (peace be upon him). Whilst saying that, I am not disputing the undeniable fact that there were still immeasurable treasures of wisdom to learn and enjoy from the lives and sayings of the learned, whether they be respected companions of the Prophet, or the many learned 'revivers' of faith and knowledge whom God inspired to provide light to the seekers. Each would respect the knowledge and status of the other even if they differed. I too, wanted to maintain my beautiful vision of the original unity in Islam from the Prophet's closest companion, Abu Bakr *Al Siddiq*, to Abu Hanifah and Imam Ghazali, even if they lived apart by a thousand years.

There were a variety of modern scholars whose books impressed me, especially the famous European convert Muhammad Asad. They seemed able to explain and open the door to understanding Islam in the modern context. In addition, there were other celebrated 'doctors of the heart' and the spiritual path of those who had renounced the attractions of the world, like Rumi and such, whose book, *Mathnawi*, I had been given even before I received the Qur'an. Though I met certain Sufi groups, and whilst they were extremely attractive for some new converts, I was just happy to learn and be friends with all who bowed to God and I certainly didn't want to join any group nor make enemies of anybody in the universal brotherhood of Islam.

Eventually these pressures drove me to devote myself more enthusiastically to learning basic classical Arabic and the study of the Qur'an and the Prophet's *Sunnah*, being the primary sources to which all the knowledgeable throughout history have deferred. With the patient and kind assistance of my Arabic teacher from Tunisia, Shaikh Tijani, I began learning the meaning of all the chapters I was able to memorize from the Qur'an.

Nevertheless, to repeat, I feel no hesitation in admitting the debt we all, as students, owe to the great bodies of work and canons of interpretation and jurisprudence from those authoritative teachers of Divine knowledge. They spent their lives in the service of God, studying the Qur'an and *Sunnah* and bequeathing their huge legacy of wisdom to the world, may Allah be pleased with them all. Without them the civilization of Islam and the development of the Muslim world and its contribution to law, science, medicine, ethics, philosophy and so many disciplines would not have shone for all mankind – by the grace of Allah.

In reality, all of the famous founders of Islamic thought who served the *Khilafah*[31] would uphold the basic principle that whenever there exists a Qur'anic verse or an authentic saying of the Prophet (peace be upon him) then, 'that is my way (*madhhab*)'.

> **O ye who believe! Obey Allah, and obey the Messenger, and those charged with authority among you. If ye differ in anything among yourselves, refer it to Allah and His Messenger, if ye do believe in Allah and the Last Day: That is best, and most suitable for final determination.**[32]

TROUBLE

Then the world changed; along came the Iranian Revolution – a new Islamic political order had arrived and the world trembled, big time! The West shook violently from the reverberations of this new, unforeseen Islamic uprising. Relative disinterest about passive 'oriental Islam' faded overnight. Forget what I said about not wanting to make enemies, they were already made for me. Suddenly Muslims were painted black, turbaned (or veiled) and militant; the media had a blitzkrieg.

This happened one short year after I had entered Islam. It was a time when there was no grey area left: it was black or white. Either you applauded the downfall of the puppet Shah, or you derided the new breed of theological autocrats – the Ayatollahs. The press, naturally, had quite a party.

I was dismayed to see the image of Islam portrayed like a horror movie, swathes of angry looking Muslims every night on the BBC's *Nine O'Clock News*, chanting and cursing the West. My situation altered drastically; from being one of the majority, I was now in a minority.

Almost unnoticeably, a wall was being built around us; we were thrown into the shadows of a long and dark night.

One tragic and world-shaking disaster after another followed: the Iran – Iraq War, leaving a million dead; Afghanistan invaded by the Soviets; Palestinians abandoned, fighting for survival and cultural preservation in their own homeland; famines, floods, earthquakes, the bad news began to rush in like waves, day after day. New conflicts and wars were hatched with frightening regularity. Muslims were incited to fight each other over the sanctity of territorial lines drawn up by politicians and bespectacled foreign civil servants, using gold-tipped pens, from Britain, France, Russia, the US and every other triumphant nation that left their mark after the fall of the Ottoman caliphate.

Please, someone remind me what planet I am on? The call to create peace and unity, which I gleaned from the Qur'an, and the example of the Prophet (peace be upon him) was nowhere to be seen.

And if two parties of believers fall to fighting, then make peace between them. [33]

In the light of the Qur'anic injunction to 'Work together for righteousness and piety', I did whatever I could, at least to try and bring together disparate Muslim organizations in the UK to cooperate in charity work. Together with other prominent Muslim leaders (including Dr Darsh) we developed a constitution for a new charity organization called Muslim Aid. I was subsequently appointed its first chairman in 1985.

Using whatever independent collateral I had (including my own *Zakat*), my simple objective was to unite and focus energy on good deeds of charity – especially considering the amount of orphans being created through the terrible wars and conflicts. There were certainly enough causes and disasters, but never enough time, money or long-term planning to solve them.

> 'The clouds of ignorance were gathering above us. The work of calling people to enter peace through the worship of one God, was still unattended on a major scale.'

Invitations to speak at universities and gatherings from all round the world bombarded my secretary's desk every day. Each audience gave me a warm enthusiastic reception; they all seemed to be inspired by listening to my story of how I came to Islam. These meetings were mostly attended by Muslims and it felt like I was being treated a bit like a mascot, paraded with pride in front of crowds of admirers – not very different from the old days of fans and adoration. Fortunately I didn't need a band, stage engineers or managers anymore. Because of my music fame, oftentimes I would be asked to sing a couple of lines *a cappella* (with voice only) on a very cheap microphone. Sometimes I would consent and sing a song I wrote for my first child, Hasanah, called 'A is for Allah'.

Now the father of five children, I joined together with other like-minded Muslim parents, embarking on a struggle to remove the prejudice and barriers within the education system in UK. As British taxpayers and citizens, we sought equality for our Muslim Primary School, Islamia (which I had founded in 1983), to be recognized and supported along with the already flourishing Christian and Jewish schools up and down the country. Islamia Primary School was a forerunner, one of the first professional full-time Muslim schools in Britain and, as my trust had paid for the building and covered the shortfall in running costs, predictably perhaps, the parents and governors pushed me forward to act – again – as chairman and public spokesperson.

It was a major challenge, but one I felt was vital to take on; the cause of Muslim schools was the most important because it meant the tacit recognition of Islam as a home-grown faith in Britain. There was no constitution to guarantee Muslims rights, except those found in the European Convention on Human Rights, which were not binding. I realized that there could never be a home for Islam in Europe without a solid educational base for our children. This led to the formation of IBERR, an international board of educational research and resources for Islamic schools that developed materials and guidelines for the establishment of Muslim schools worldwide.

While we were struggling to educate our offspring and give them a better chance in life, the clouds of ignorance were gathering above us. The work of calling people to enter peace through the worship of one God, was still unattended on a major scale. More mosques were being built in Europe and alarm bells were beginning to ring for those who saw this as an encroachment on traditional Western culture and values; certain gatekeepers saw Islam like some 'heathen' culture of alien beliefs in crescents and stars, false deities and lovers of war.

1989: in rides the not-quite-so-white knight, Rushdie and his satanic verses as a long awaited 'secularist-saviour', to rescue the hopes of the establishment under a thinly cloaked disguise of 'freedom of speech' (if they really knew how many times he swore and cursed the British establishment, the royal family and degraded women in his book they might have thought twice). No one seemed to be thinking straight in those highly-charged rallying days of – dare I say it – 'fire and brimstone'. I also got dragged into the debate.

A *fatwah* was issued on behalf of Ayatollah Khomeini; this turned out to be a death edict on the author. When asked about the *fatwah* (literally: a legal opinion), what I actually did was to provide a generic textbook response, confirming that, according to my research, blasphemy was a major sin and a capital offence in Islam, exactly the same way as it was a capital offence in Judaism and Christianity, according to the Torah and Gospel.[34] To deny that would be like denying the existence of the sun on a cloudless summer's day.

However, the *fatwah* went further than repeating the obvious, stating it was a heavenly duty on every 'zealous' Muslim to seek to kill the author of the book! This was to be an enormous test, especially for someone like me who was invited to the front line to explain Islam's position. Confused, the only place I could go for guidance was to the scholars. Thanks to the strong and balanced research by certain Imams, including Dr Darsh, it was clear that the *fatwah* was in no way applicable and that Muslims have a moral obligation to follow the laws of the country in which they live, provided the government does not force them to cease the practice of Islam or their worship and fundamental obligations to God. Lawlessness and vigilantism are inimical to Islam and not allowed. This was included clearly in my press release at the time, but the media conveniently ignored my statement and mischievously went on to make up their own.[35]

I was soon targeted for not siding with a fellow 'artist' and supporting freedom of speech, yet... hang on a minute, my songs were being banned from radio stations in the US and my records crushed under a steamroller! Interesting that freedom of speech should only be fully accepted from those who want to vilify religion but not extended to those who believe in it. No way! That would be a cardinal sin according to the sacred scrolls of secular philosophy. 'Let there be freedom', bellowed the voice of the great editor sitting above the white puffy clouds. Next came the headlines, 'Cat Says Kill Rushdie.'

Angry and frustrated I foolishly agreed to take part in a television show that posed loaded hypothetical questions from an expert QC.

'9/11... The manic attempt to cause maximum suffering and death in the name of Islam now became the greatest opportunity to blacken the name of Muslims you could ever dream of.'

During that programme many things were said. I tried to bring in a bit of British sarcasm but they edited out my rational arguments and only included the sensational and dotty stuff. 'Let that bit be heard', commanded the great editor in the clouds. The other comments were laid to rest on the editing floor.[36]

The truth of the matter is that I never agreed with the *fatwah*, in fact, I firmly believe it went against the basic injunction in Islam which forbids the taking of life without just right – lawfully – part of due process in maintaining law and order within society. Never did I say, 'Kill Rushdie' or believe that Muslims were morally or duty bound to take the law into their own hands or support vigilantism of any kind.

The raging battle for 'freedom' and the assertion of godless values created a dangerous atmosphere and was followed closely by a new phase, raising the ghosts of Christian extremism and hostility towards Muslims, and memories of former religious witch-hunts in Europe – this time under another name: Islamophobia.

This new terrifying phenomenon paved the way for unimaginable crimes and massacres to be carried out under the devilish policy of 'ethnic cleansing' in Kosovo and Bosnia-Herzegovina and was probably the turning point for me. Watching helplessly, as politicians dithered and delayed, while Muslims were slaughtered, their houses and mosques burnt and pillaged, women raped on Europe's doorstep – Oh God! What else could go wrong?

Whilst these Muslim communities were besieged, pounded daily by devastating military forces, the name of Islam was being dragged through the gutter by the media.

Anger within young radical circles was reaching volatile levels, yet no matter how bad things were getting, prophetic etiquette teaches that it should never lead Muslims to extremities either. Unfortunately, that's just what happened. We didn't have to wait too long.

9/11: The atrocious attack against innocent civilians, men women and children shook us all, alike. The manic attempt to cause maximum suffering and death in the name of Islam now became the greatest opportunity to blacken the name of Muslims you could ever dream of, perpetrated by people who were claiming to work for God. Offering a new excuse for the 'powers that be' to settle old scores and (following the dismantling of the USSR and the major 'Red' threat to the Western world) to ramp up attacks on Muslim majority and minority heartlands, setting off a whole new unending war against the faith of Muslims. Stop! In God's good name – I wanted to scream.

THE CALL

What was so depressingly sad was that the heavenly call to the peace and prosperity of Islam had been lost in the clamour and confusion created by that terrorist attack. The lofty ethical objective and God-consciousness was hijacked by those who saw themselves as the self-appointed liberators of the oppressed Muslims of the world. What they did in fact, was an even greater disservice, by allowing right-wing politicians as well as Islamophobic press and media institutions to be more successful, turning Islam into an unrecognizable distortion of the original universal order and blessing ordained by God for the benefit and peace of mankind, delivered by the beloved Prophet (peace be upon him). Islam, as a result, was demoted in the eyes of the world to the level of anarchic groups, bent on the destruction of Western civilization, willing to sacrifice themselves as well as innocent bystanders for the cause.

This opened the doors to an armageddon. Gross injustices increased, persecution and killing ensued. Afghanistan became a prime target, followed next by Iraq on the basis of the spurious accusation of holding 'Weapons of Mass Destruction'. It was a lie. But discovered too late, now a massive well-equipped, well-prepared war machine had begun to roll over Muslim lands, one by one. The true cause of *Da'wah*, the imperative, following the example of the Prophet, was ignored in the rush to commence *jihad* by splinter groups and movements, oftentimes fighting against each other.

'Preach on my behalf, even if it is only one verse,'[37] said the Prophet (peace be upon him). Good sense tells us that this should obviously not start with a *Madani* verse[38] taken out of context, about fighting or right to retaliation; it should commence with a much higher and universal ideal. Justice and wisdom demand that a person puts first things first. Ironically, at almost every mosque on Friday, the Imam usually ends his sermon by repeating the primary command to be just and good:

> **Verily! Allah orders justice and kindness and giving to relatives, and forbids lewdness, bad conduct and oppression. Allah instructs you that perhaps you may be reminded.** [39]

Denying the existence of Allah, glorified is He above all, worshipping others and making partners with Him, has been stated by the Prophet as the greatest injustice. So enjoining mankind to enter belief (*Iman*) and worship of the one true Lord and Creator and Owner of the Universe, and reminding people of the Day of Judgement, is the first and foremost duty in whatever time and space. This should also be accompanied by good character and behaviour. Not performing this noble duty and ignoring the power of education, social interaction and the media to emancipate people from the chains of ignorance will just keep the planet spinning on the Ferris wheel of war, bloodletting and revenge. Muslims should know better.

This absence of Divine knowledge and its communication (*Da'wah*) is one of the main reasons, I believe, for the failure to escape destruction and injustice being heaped on the underprivileged, peace-loving, innocent Muslims in the name of 'war against terror'. Unfortunately, it seems the prophecies by the Prophet of the approach of the Last Day are all too clearly being witnessed. He said, 'Religious ignorance will spread, knowledge will disappear there will be much killing.' [40]

Even though the Prophet and the first community of Muslims were ridiculed and persecuted under the threat of death, the Prophet worked day and night, ceaselessly to convey the words of God to the people; to teach them the oneness of Allah and to do good works of kindness, patience and charity.

Muslims should be familiar with the history of the Prophet (peace be upon him), when he journeyed to *Taif* to deliver to them the message of Islam, they replied by stoning and abusing him. Even while he was wounded and bleeding, this never deterred him or made him vengeful. Instead the Prophet prayed that in future, the children of this generation of town-dwellers may become more generous and open to the call.

Only when his violent enemies threatened the fledgling community of faithful in Madinah, after fourteen long years of passive resistance, was he allowed to fight to defend Islam militarily – and even then it was face to face, certainly not behind masks or by leaving bombs in bags.

If some Muslims believe that they can change the world and make Islam great again by blowing themselves up and taking blameless people with them, not even giving them a chance to hear the wonderfully liberating message of God and His Prophet, they have surely strayed far, far away. There is no room for collateral damage in an honourable and just war. Even in the days of the Prophet and his companions, when they were commanded to defend Islam against the violent attacks of the polytheists and their allies, they always left room for their enemies to hear the word of God and embrace Islam and the old, the women, children and even trees were always left unharmed.

Socrates is reported to have inspired the saying, 'Ignorance is the root of all evil'. No matter whose saying that is, it's a wise one. It is an indisputable fact that knowledge is the first key to practising Islam

'Back in 1994 I tried, in my small way, to correct the imbalance by launching a record label called Mountain of Light.'

and to the correct behaviour for a Muslim. Imagine not giving the chance for someone ignorant about Islam to be killed in its name. This is the greatest injustice and must be condemned as a complete aberration of Islam and its enlightened Divine objectives.

> **O ye who believe! When you go forth (to fight) in the way of Allah, be careful to discriminate, and say not unto one who offers you peace: 'Thou art not a believer,' seeking the chance profits of this life. With Allah are plenteous spoils. Even thus (as he now is) were you before; but Allah has since then been gracious unto you. Therefore take care to discriminate. Allah is ever Informed of what you do.** [41]

As John Lennon once said, 'You may say I'm a dreamer, but I'm not the only one.' The middle ground needs to rise again; the people of knowledge and moderation have to regain the original vision of making the world a happier place for all. That cannot happen without a better lesson plan. For well over three decades, I have tried to help the cause of education and improve the image of Islam. The Islamic Circle we started at the London Central Mosque is still being held every Saturday; hundreds have accepted Islam at the Circle – thanks to God. It is clear that when people get in touch with the pure, undistorted call to one God and His last Prophet, the situation can change; but outside these small limited circles, large negative headlines continue to dominate the news.

As it is well known, the majority of the media is under the control of those who don't know or often prefer to misrepresent the faith of Islam. Back in 1994 I tried, in my small way to correct the imbalance by launching a record label called Mountain of Light, going back into the studio to produce a recording of *The Life of the Last Prophet* (peace be upon him). For me it was the first time I stepped into a recording studio since I left the music business. Though my spoken-word album wasn't a 'smash hit' in the West, it was in Turkey, where it sold a million. This paved the way for me and others to raise the volume, quality and authenticity of the message to a more acceptable level and show Muslims that we can use freedom, resources and ability to make a better impression with a story that we know so well.

Tala 'al badru 'alayna
Min thaniyat Al wada
Wajaba shukru 'alayna
Ma da'a lillahi da'

Oh the white moon rose over us
From the valley of Wada'
And we owe it to show gratefulness
Where the Call is to Allah. [42]

RETURN TO DA'WAH THROUGH HARMONY

At the beginning of the new millennium, millions of people were driven away from Islam by the terrible news bloodying the front pages every day. After 9/11, the importance of giving the good news of the Prophet, for me, was even more urgent and vital.

Hey, didn't I once write a song called 'Peace Train'?! It's good to remember (and some Muslims seem to forget this point) that the word Islam finds its root in the word, *Salam,* which means peace and security – how far we had drifted. That was when I realized that it was time to raise my voice again.

> 'Cause out on the edge of darkness
> There rides a Peace Train
> O, Peace Train take this country
> Come take me home again. [43]

Those lyrics I wrote as Cat Stevens could easily have been written by a Muslim. This brings to mind a *Hadith*: after hearing the poetry of Umayya son of Abi Alsalt, the Prophet (peace be upon him) said, 'He (Umayya) was close to becoming a Muslim'. On another occasion he said, 'He was almost a Muslim in his poetry.' [44]

The truth is that I have gradually softened my objections to making music and songs over the years, and there are at least four good reasons:

The fact that I have studied the subject carefully in the Qur'an and sayings and actions of the Prophet (peace be upon him). I have not just adopted the *fatwah* of a school of thought, without questioning the interpretation of texts by renowned scholars, no matter how well-meaning, who took a negative view and disapproved of it. Instead, I accepted the more positive, less restrictive view, also supported by numerous scholars, which I believe is the stronger of the two opinions.

Secondly, my faith was stronger: I was certainly not going back to what they call 'Sex, Drugs, Rock & Roll'. My life was no longer hostage to the main attractions and corruptive influences of the music business thanks to Islam; my intention was to use music for positive purposes, good news based on *Istihsan*.[45]

Thirdly, considering time and context, ever since the ghastly genocide against Bosnian Muslims in the heart of Europe, I learnt how important motivational songs were for keeping people's spirits high during times of great calamity. This is in keeping with the example of the Prophet (peace be upon him). He is once reported to have silenced Umar Ibn Al Khatab's objections while hearing some poetry on a particular expedition and said that the poetry of Abdullah Ibn Rawahah was '...stronger than a hundred arrows.' [46] In the science of *Fiqh* it is also acknowledged that 'circumstances dictate exceptions'.

'Music is universally present in this world, even in the jungles, oceans and deserts, birds sing, seas crash, and the wind howls. Nature has its own magnificent song in praise of the Creator.'

Finally, the reality is that music is played everywhere. Even in the two sacred precincts (*Harams*) – the House of God in Makkah and the Prophet's Mosque in Madinah, there are hotels and shops providing piped music, TV programmes and mobile phone ringtones, all within earshot of the blessed worshippers. If music and its practical uses was really forbidden by the Qur'an, *Hadith* and absolute consensus of scholars (*Ijma'*), then – like alcohol – it would certainly never be present in the Holy cities under the watchful eyes of the strict religious authorities – mobile phones would have to be confiscated and TV and speakers broken as would beer and wine bottles.

The fact is that music is universally present in this world, even in the jungles, oceans and deserts; birds sing, seas crash and the wind howls. Nature has its own magnificent song in praise of the Creator.

The Faith of Islam, because of its depth and breadth, and being based on the true, innate nature of humanity, was able to historically spread and accommodate all people from all cultures. The fact that Islam was able to take root in so many diverse ethnic nations is proof of the wisdom inherent in its tolerant attitude to customs and languages – as long as they do not contravene basic Islamic laws and norms. *'Urf* is the Arabic term, which in Islamic jurisprudence refers to traditions and customs of people, and can even be used as a source of law in areas left open to interpretation and *Ijtihad*.[47]

So, Islam spread through India and the South East Asian islands, largely through the good behaviour of the Muslim travellers and traders, and the development and circulation of God-conscious songs and poetry, in the language of the people.

The so-called 'golden era' of Baghdad and Islamic Spain offered glaring and historical examples of how the Muslim system of *Khilafah*[48] maintained a balanced command of law and freedom for its subjects, keeping within the bounds of *Shari'ah* whilst expanding the lands of Islam. The fifth Abbassid *Khalifah*, Harun Al Rashid, was a great patron of the arts, music and literature. His library in Baghdad was the largest in the world; it was during his reign that *One Thousand and One Nights* was written and compiled. This is still known today as one of the most imaginative and influential novels ever published, still exploited to this day by Disney.

Thanks to the academic research of Professor Salim Al Hassani and his brilliant work, *1001 Inventions*, I discovered another important fact. Late in eighth-century Islamic Spain lived an extraordinary Muslim endowed with myriad talents called Ziryab: he was a courtier, a poet, a musician, singer, astronomer, chemist, geographer and strategist. According to records Ziryab is credited as having introduced and improved the *'Oud* (the lute – the father of guitars) by adding a fifth string and was a great influence on Spanish music and the Andalusian music traditions of North Africa. So the Blues and Rock and Roll probably owe Ziryab some credit.

> 'We were being overridden by hip-hop culture, sexual commerce and fashion, which did not correspond to our vision of the 'good life', where faith, love of family, children and respect within society should reign.'

Evaluating the bleak reality of the situation in the world today made me realize that as representatives of Islam, especially those who speak the English language, we desperately need to revive and recirculate Islam's powerful spiritual and cultural values back into the world. We were being overridden by hip-hop culture, sexual commerce and fashion, which did not correspond to our vision of the 'good life', where faith, love of family, children and respect within society should reign.

Muslims at one time – in fact, for a thousand years – were the most civilized and advanced. Science, astronomy, medicine, literature and art were just some of the fields in which Muslims were pioneers and excelled – all these, of course, are in addition to the amazing and meticulous religious sciences developed in the elucidation and study of the Qur'an and *Hadith*.

If we are ever to reclaim the moral high ground we need to be much more educated in the history of human civilization illuminated by the powerful prophetic light of knowledge, which fuelled the quest for health, happiness and progress in the past. Maybe we will not able to surpass the scientific advancements of present-day technology, quantum physics or space exploration, but we could certainly help people down here on earth appreciate Islam's undeniable and beneficial contribution to human life, knowledge and understanding, and teach people to rediscover the moral imperative which drives us to become better human beings as God's honoured trustees of the earth and all its creatures.

> O Very young, what will you leave us this time?
> You're only dancing on this earth for a short while
> And though your dreams may toss and turn you now,
> They will vanish away like your daddy's best jeans,
> Denim blue fading up to the sky. [49]

My songs were never wilfully immoral or without a meaning of some kind; they were about trying to understand life or make the world a nicer place. So when I returned to writing songs again it was natural for me to continue the same underlying message – strengthened now through faith and knowledge of Islam.

Going through the communications and letters we've received in our office and on the website over the years, it's clear that some of my songs have helped many people, including those who were depressed and on the verge of suicide, to see life in a positive light again, and others who have accepted and embraced Islam. Allah says, 'Whoever saves the life of one human being it is as if he has saved the whole of humanity'. [50]

As I look back at my life, it is clear that as Cat Stevens – the reclusive, hippy poet – I was gifted with an ability to write music and words that inspired people and made them think about life. It was part of God's plan for me. Now was the time to help those rather perplexed people

I left behind – non-Muslims and now, Muslims – to carry on with my 'specialization' and enable people to realize that Islam does not forbid what is good and meaningful in art and music; it simply does not sanction what is vile, mindless or vain.

> How great the wonders of the heavens
> And the timeless beauty of the night
> How Great? Then how great the Creator
> And its stars like priceless jewels
> High above the reach of kings
> Bow down for the shepherd guiding him home. [51]

CHILDREN AND SONG

In a famous incident recorded in *Sahih Al Bukhari*, the blessed Prophet (peace be upon him) did not object whilst the songs of *Jahiliyyah* (society of ignorance) were being sung in his presence. Aisha (may Allah be pleased with her) reported that her father came to the house of the Prophet while he was resting and two small Ansari girls were singing a famous battle song about the Tribes of 'Aus' and 'Khazraj', commemorating the Day of Bu'ath (before Islam). Her father was shocked and protested, 'Musical instruments of Satan in the house of Allah's Messenger!' But Allah's Messenger said, 'O Abu Bakr! There is an *'Eid* (festive enjoyment) for every nation and this is our *'Eid.*' [52] There is also another report that during the *'Eid,* the Prophet (peace be upon him) said, 'Let the Jews of Madinah know that our Religion is spacious (and has room for flexibility) and I have been sent with an easy and straightforward religion.' [53]

These *Hadith* are very important because firstly they are highly authentic and secondly, they clearly show the direct response of the Prophet (peace be upon him) related to this subject of music and songs, through his actions – as well as his wife's – in the Prophet's house.

In *fiqh* it is acknowledged that *Hadith,* which embodies the witnessed actions of the Prophet are weightier than those which are just reported 'speech', for example, those which say, 'I heard the Messenger of Allah say...' – and Allah knows best.

Coming back to present times, it is a fact that in today's world, whether in a social context or working environment, every day has been made into an opportunity or occasion for fun and enjoyment. Music and entertainment are astonishingly almost everywhere! In schools, shops, malls, dental practices, hospitals, cafes, on TV, radio, mobile phones, internet, we are exposed 24/7 to a relentless barrage of sound and songs, most of it pushing hip-hop, immature and hedonistic messages onto an unsuspecting public.

Being concerned with education and the upbringing of children, it was clear that I had to employ my talents to reach the hearts of the next generation; many were getting lost and gradually turning away from Islam. This was also a result of strict and stern-faced 'Islamic' teachers, who were employed to teach them Qur'an and Islam – mostly after school. They made many students dislike the subject of Islam because it was mainly based on memorization; repeating rules without explanation or meaning. Muslim boys and girls were being hit from both sides: their non-Muslim friends laughed at them because they couldn't enjoy the same freedoms and pleasures as them, while some Islamic teachers were punishing them for not doing well enough in their Islamic studies.

So, over the years following on from *The Life of the Last Prophet,* for parents who wanted to offer their children an alternative, I had produced a few children's CDs and publications; the first of which included my alphabet song and book called *A is for Allah.* Many Muslim children living in the West benefited from these early works; perhaps these were some of the first Islamic *Nasheeds* (motivational songs) available and recorded in the English language. Children loved them. They sang and learnt about Islam at the same time. The demands for helping the new generation learn Islam were great – and they are still growing.

> A is for Allah, nothing but Allah
> B is the beginning of Bismillah
> T is for Taqwa, bewaring of Allah, and
> Th is for Thawab, a reward. [54]

Again, I remember in the early days of the conflict in Bosnia, one Egyptian doctor working on the ground phoned me from Sarajevo and pleaded with me to use my voice for children who were being slaughtered and maimed. That inspired me to write, 'The Little Ones'. Following the horrific incident in a Scottish school I renamed it, 'The Little Ones (of Sarajevo and Dunblane)'.

> O they've killed all the Little Ones
> With their eyes open wide
> There was no one to help them,
> On the day that they died
> No bed to run under; no cupboard to hide. [55]

The tragedy of the Bosnian war also helped me discover a whole new genre of Islamic European music. Whilst working for Muslim Aid and providing support to the orphans and families in the Balkans, I met the then Bosnian Foreign Secretary, Dr Irfan Ljubijankić, who had written a Bosnian song called 'I Have No Cannons That Roar'. Dr Irfan's song, the melody and words, were so moving, I was strongly affected. When we heard that he was shot down in a helicopter while flying over the hills of Bosnia, it made me realize I had to do something with Dr Irfan's song.

> I have no cannons that roar
> But I have faith in God and love
> And I'll surrender you to no one else
> My Mother, Bosnia, my love. [56]

'The fact that this was an Arab state ... offering such a broad and tolerant environment, made it irresistible for me.'

We produced an album of Bosnian and English songs called *I Have No Cannons That Roar*. Some of the artists, like Dino Merlin, used instruments, and at that time I was not using them personally on my recordings. I was still staying away from guitars and pianos following the view I initially adopted against the use of musical instruments.

But I was becoming less and less convinced about the arguments commonly used against music and its benefits. Whilst the equilibrium of the world was in jeopardy and Muslims were being blown to bits and killed by guns and bombs, surely words and music that help people to learn the message and culture of Islam were not harmful but beneficial. It was the President of Bosnia and Herzegovina himself, Dr Alia Izetbegovic, who personally requested that I take up music again, to help bridge the enormous cultural gap – particularly in Europe where music is part of the everyday air that people live and breathe.

After the Dayton Peace Agreement for Bosnia and Herzegovina and the final lifting of the siege of Sarajevo, I was invited to perform at a celebratory concert in the city itself. For the first time in seventeen years I climbed the stage and began to sing. Though I nervously sang to the accompaniment of only a simple duff [57] in my hand, the reception was thunderous; the President was also in the audience, obviously pleased.

It was becoming clear how powerful music was; raising hearts and delivering a hopeful message.

As soon as we began developing and producing this new genre of Islamic song in English, a whole new movement of writers and singers emerged: Raihan, Sami Yusuf, Native Deen, Zain Bhikha, and Ahmed Bukhatir. The ground was beginning to rumble with the reverberation of inspiring and Muslim-friendly music.

Then I heard rumour of a new Media City project in Dubai, a modern metropolis that was fast developing as a centre of communication and business in the Middle East. So I decided to open the Mountain of Light office there in 2001. The UAE, and Dubai particularly, was growing day by day with more and more skyscraper offices and housing projects. The fact that this was an Arab state with mosques everywhere (even inside shopping malls), offering such a broad and tolerant environment, made it irresistible for me, particularly as the sun seemed to shine like summer every day – how delightful! I rented a villa and together with my family and creative team, started to work on what would become one of the most successful children's albums in English, *I Look I See*, produced with the help of our close friends and partners in South Africa.

> I look, I look, I look, I see
> I see a world of beauty
> I touch, I touch, I touch, I feel
> I feel the world around so real
> And everything I do
> I dedicate to You
> Cause You made me; I am for you. [58]

A GUITAR COMES HOME

Something quite unexpected and profound happened in 2002: my son, Muhammad, had bought himself a guitar and brought it back into the house. It was an important crossroads for me; doubts about musical instruments being *haram* were now much weightier in my opinion and could not just be swept under the carpet anymore. Everything going on around required me to re-evaluate my position. I certainly didn't lose my temper or get angry with him about the guitar, which I would have done at one time. Instead, one quiet morning in Dubai while everyone else in the villa was sleeping, I picked up the guitar and began to play. Soon after writing a new song and contemplating the issue, I realized that perhaps I had another job to do.

A young son had come home and unwittingly reminded his father that it was time for him to change. Whoa! Wasn't that the subject of a song I once wrote called 'Father & Son'?

It was clear that I needed to be courageous and decisive based on my knowledge of Islam, and not to be overly concerned about the back-talk of others. Doing that would have made me a slave to people's opinions (no matter how nice or pious those people were) and forced me to ignore the certainty which Allah's Book inspired within me.

'I picked up the guitar
and began to play.
Soon after writing
a new song and
contemplating the issue,
I realized that perhaps
I had another job to do.'

Naturally, when I was new to Islam there was good reason to be cautious, but I had spent many years studying the influences of Islamic thought on the unity of the Muslim world, and realized that there was more harm if people simply inherited their religion and opinions and abandoned the need for *Ijtihad* (intellectual struggle) in dealing directly with the problems faced in this rapidly degenerating world. Never had the people of this blessed earth ever experienced such an atheistically secular and godless age – this was the true challenge of our time.

I had studied many interpretations and arguments over the years very closely, and in the end I realized that in this matter – as with all matters – the judgement rests only with Allah and His Messenger, they alone had the absolute right to be obeyed. After all these years, even with all the diverse opinions within the theological community, past and present, I returned to the clear foundations of the Qur'an and authentic sayings, actions and silent approvals of the Prophet (peace be upon him). There was not enough undisputed evidence in Islam's original scriptural sources of Divine knowledge to support the complete banning of music from human life and its objectives. For me it was not turning away from Islam; it was facing it in the twenty-first century with new inspiration and vision based on the eternal foundations provided by Allah in the Qur'an.

> Say: 'Who has forbidden the beautiful [gifts] of Allah which He has brought forth for His servants and the good things of His providing?' Say: 'Such, on the Day of Resurrection, will be only for those who believed during the life of the world.' Thus do We detail Our revelations for people who have knowledge.
>
> Say: 'My Lord forbids only indecencies, such of them as are apparent and such as are within; and sin and wrongful oppression; and [He has forbidden] that you associate with Allah that for which no warrant has been revealed; and that you tell concerning Allah that which you know not.' [59]

Unquestioningly following the dictates of scholars and founders of various schools of thought, whilst they may be some of the most eminent and devoted Muslims who have ever striven to serve Islam (we pray they are blessed by Allah for serving the *Ummah*) through their work and developing the noble science of *Usul al Fiqh*,[60] was not what my heart and mind understood from the Glorious Qur'an in matters of obedience. There was a verse in direct connection to this in the Qur'an:

> O you who believe! Obey Allah and His Messenger, and turn not away from him when you hear (him speak). Be not as those who say, we hear, and they hear not. [61]

The fact that there was no clear, unambiguous verse in the Qur'an specifically mentioning the word 'music' (there is no such word in Arabic) added to the fact that there were numerous authentic *Hadith* which show the Prophet's distance – by virtue of his silence – from issuing an unequivocal and direct prohibition or command about this broad issue we call 'music', was precisely the reason why scholars over the years have made *fatawa* (legal opinions) about it. It is to be mentioned here that there is no need for a *fatwah* when a matter has been clearly stated by Allah and His Prophet, (peace be upon him); a *fatwah* in Arabic and juristic terms means, literally, an opinion. Take alcohol, gambling, suicide, cheating, usury or fornication for example – you don't need a scholar to give you a legal opinion regarding these, all mentioned clearly in the Qur'an as well as *Hadith* as *haram* (prohibited).

The closest we come in reference to music in the Qur'an is under the broad meaning of the word *'Lahw'* which means entertainment, a pastime activity or diversion. Those who hold that music is *haram* usually quote this sixth verse from the Qur'an in Surah Luqman:

> **But there are among men those who purchase idle tales (*lahw-hadeeth*) without knowledge or meaning, to mislead men from the path of God and throw ridicule on the path – for such there will be a humiliating penalty. When Our signs are rehearsed to such a one, he turns away in arrogance as if he heard them not, as if there was deafness in both his ears. Announce to him a grievous penalty.** [62]

Quite apart from the terminology, which does not mention music, the context of this verse has to be studied as it is vital to the understanding of the warning given in this particular verse. In the books of *tafsir* (Qur'anic interpretation) and *Hadith* it is reported that this verse was revealed about a man who purposefully had bought a singing slave girl to entertain and divert people away from listening to the message of the Prophet (peace be upon him) and put them off following the path of God – generally making a mockery of Islam. Well, let's be absolutely honest, no one in their right mind can argue that the intention and use of a singer and the song in that situation are not blatantly sinful and blameworthy, clearly *haram* – there is no argument about that.

There is a strong statement by Ibn Mas'ud who swore that this verse refers to 'singing'. But this may be understood as a 'specific' (*khas*) explanation based on and related to this specific incident about the man who bought a singer to intentionally divert people from listening to the Qur'an – again, nothing contested about that, but it would be highly irregular if the verse implied a complete 'general' (*'aam*) prohibition of singing as that would suggest that the Prophet – as reported in *Hadith* on many occasions – did not observe a prohibition, Allah forbid!

A general prohibition of *Lahw* is not what the verse intends – Allah knows best – because we can see from an incident reported in *Sahih* collection of *Hadith* where the Prophet actually mentioned *Lahw* in a positive sense and encouraged that there should be such entertainment at weddings for people to enjoy.[63]

Then we come to a second Qur'anic verse, which is cited as evidence against singing and music, referring to the voice of Satan (*Shaytan*):

And excite any of them whom you (Satan) can with your voice, and urge your horse and foot against them, and be a partner in their wealth and children, and promise them. Satan promises them only to deceive. [64]

Again we can see that music is not mentioned, only the 'voice' of Satan. It is well known that Satan whispers suggestions into the hearts of men to disobey Allah and to sin. This is not disputed, but to attribute the use of that 'voice' to singers and songs (whilst in the case of songs which encourage disobedience it is totally understood, as with reference to the singing girl who was purchased to mislead people from hearing and following the truth) and yet not to equally extend the interpretation to Satan's incitement to disobedience and sin through the instruments of fortune tellers, politicians, religious fanatics, storytellers, philosophers, warmongers, adulterers, cheats or racists, clearly seems to limit what is intended – and Allah knows best.

Therefore we have tried to show that the verses of the Qur'an which are used to support the ban of singing and songs can have more than one interpretation or meaning and in no verse does the Qur'an clearly and unambiguously forbid Muslims from singing or reciting harmless words (with or without accompaniment). And so we inevitably end up arriving at the door of *Hadith*.

Whilst I am certainly not claiming to be a scholar, after twenty-five years of studying the subject, I became aware that many of the *Hadith* which were used to prohibit music altogether are not clear in the authentic collections, and even one reference in *Sahih Al Bukhari*[65] is lodged under the heading of 'Drink' and had a broken chain (*munqati*); in addition, there are other anomalies to this *Hadith*[66] as well as there being several versions of it[67] with different words and emphasis (and therefore – changing or altering the meaning away from being specifically considered *haram*).

After my son confronted me with the dilemma of the guitar I reviewed all these deliberated matters. I personally concluded that listening to music, attending musical gatherings, or studying music of all genres and instruments, as far as I gathered from the Qur'anic and prophetic evidences, may be allowed as long as it is not accompanied by immoral and sinful acts, mocking belief in God, or used as a pretext to incite people towards *haram* (prohibited) behaviour, and it does not preoccupy a person away from observing the obligatory acts of worship – a principle which could of course apply to any other activity from horse riding to cooking or preparing for exams.

But please understand, it is not my role to pass a *fatwah*, nor am I expected to do so. I am not claiming to be sinless; I am personally trying to explain my own actions; I try to follow the clear path of Islam, according to clear evidence, and stay away from that which Allah, the Almighty and Most Wise, has stated is inarguably and clearly forbidden.

If you avoid the major sins which you are forbidden, We will remove from you your lesser sins and admit you to a noble entrance (into Paradise). [68]

It's quite amazing to me that so many well-meaning brothers and sisters who are concerned for the upholding of what is right (*ma'ruf*) and forbidding what is immoral (*munkar*), will spend so much time on an issue like music. This is not even recognized as a subject in the major books of *Hadith*, nor is it defined as a major sin.[69] All the while, the blood of innocent men, women and children continues to flow in political wars and genocides, people are maimed and starving, Muslim countries are fighting each other over borders or religious differences, generations are drained of an economic future through interest and government mismanagement; and the majority of people (four-fifths) still don't know that God sent Muhammad as the last Messenger to mankind as a true liberator from poverty and ignorance – are there no priorities?

THE NEW WAVE

There was certainly a job to do alright. Having been away from mainstream writing and music for so long, a question high in my mind and many other people's was whether – after all these untilled years – Islam had curbed the power I had to be creative. So in a way I needed to prove something to myself, as well as to my fans and Muslims generally: that Islam did not drain my artistic abilities (or anyone else's for that matter), but inspired, heightened and guided them.

The task was becoming clearer now. The broadcasting of a TV documentary based on my life and journey called *Behind the Music*, produced by VH1 in the US in 2000, was another important turning point. It showed to a much greater degree, more than ever before, the reasons for my turning away from my old life and my experience of coming to Islam and becoming a Muslim. Yet for me it didn't go far enough; the way in which it told my story, using my songs as a soundtrack to illustrate the journey was too spiritually shallow; it made me realize how important it was to be in charge of the script.

That was when I revived the idea of writing my own musical story, based on a young optimistic soul who goes on a dangerous journey, searching

'Picking up the guitar made me feel just like I did when I first began to learn chords back in the sixties, like being an amateur again with nothing to lose; a flood of new music poured out.'

for the key to everlasting happiness – on the way he finds something quite different. Ever since I was a young lad running around the streets of London, slipping into the back doors of theatres and cinemas, I had been an admirer of musicals and always wanted to write one. My songs always painted pictures and told stories, so it was a natural medium for my art. Somehow, my path took another course and I became a pop singer.

My brother, David, who had come back to help me sort out some issues with the publishing company and contracts, was also excited by the idea and started to assist me in the planning and logistics. I began writing the script and looked for a director to cooperate with me on the project.

I worked on a tale about a boy (very much like Salman Al Farisi or 'Siddartha') who left home to find out more about life but ended up almost facing his own destruction. He's saved only by the discovery of the truth, upon which he returns home (much like the *The Alchemist,* by Paolo Coelho). Of course, it was very much based on my own life story and tentatively titled: *On the Road to Findout*.

My songwriting was beginning to flow, particularly when it came to writing new material for the musical. Picking up the guitar made me feel just like I did when I first began to learn chords back in the sixties, like being an amateur again with nothing to lose; a flood of new music poured out of me. With the help of a small cassette recorder I captured all these fresh ideas. It wasn't long before I had about ten new songs ready to go into the studio and record.

Putting the idea of the musical to one side for a while, I bumped into a man called Steve Buckingham who produced records for the legendary blues and country label, Vanguard, in the US. I accepted an open invitation to go to Nashville to make a whole album.

On 21 September 2004 I cheerily travelled with my daughter, Maymanah, on a transatlantic flight from London to Nashville via Washington. I was looking forward to returning to the US having been there only four months before to promote the work of my charity Small Kindness and visit an interfaith initiative in the White House precinct as well as the director of USAid. So it seemed a typical day, but then something quite out of the blue occurred. Somebody in the US Department of Homeland Security decided my name sounded a bit radical and put me on a 'No Fly List'. We landed unexpectedly at Bangor, Maine, near Boston and were welcomed by seven FBI officers. The next day I was separated from my daughter and put on a plane back to London!

It became front page news all over the world. CNN, BBC, Sky News, Reuters, every respected news outlet and journalist scrambled for an exclusive interview with me. It was like Cat Mania all over again. The man who wrote 'Peace Train' was being recast by the US Administration to look like he was associated with terrorism; what news!

The American public had been dealt the 'fear card', and now there was doubt about my character and intentions. God knows the real reason behind the incident – a misspelling of my name, whatever. Regardless, to me it was God's will and I didn't worry any further about it. However, I did write a song about the incident and had the support of Paul McCartney and Dolly Parton singing along with me on 'Boots & Sand'. It made a lot of people understand the whole episode from another perspective: a Cowboy Western – with a little extra spaghetti thrown in.

> I was travelling Boots and Sand
> High bound for miracle land
> Met a man called Buckingham
> (He) said, 'Jo, won't you join my band?'
> Nickel jangled in the juke box
> Bird of Nashville sang. [70]

Three months later that same year, in December 2004, when a devastating tsunami hit the islands and shores of South East Asia, I wrote and recorded a song especially for charity, called 'Indian Ocean'. Like many, I was emotionally moved seeing the pictures in the press and on TV of people frantically running for their lives from an onslaught of giant waves. Travelling with my wife to Indonesia the following month we saw the devastation first hand and were able to distribute some aid.

The recording of the single was also assisted by the generous contribution of some eminent musicians and Martin Terefe, a Swedish producer, as well as renowned Indian composer, A. R. Rahman. This was the first time I had used musical instruments after a break of twenty-five years. We released the song as an internet download for orphans in Banda Aceh affected by the tsunami.

The connection with the tumultuous wave of the tsunami was instinctive; I remembered how Allah saved me from drowning in the Pacific Ocean, and here, in the South-East Asian islands, thousands had no chance against the mammoth onslaught of the ocean. It seemed as if there was a new chance to serve Islam by doing what I used to do so naturally – to make people concerned about the world we share and consider their obligation towards others in times of calamity. Of course, we also dispatched resources from my charity Small Kindness to assist the orphans and families affected.

'Indian Ocean' was not a massive hit but it showed that my ability to write a good song had not disappeared. A lot of people were highly thrilled that my voice still sounded the same (if maybe a quarter of a tone lower), and the music and melodies were still there.

> Suddenly I gazed up, upon a rising wave
> I saw the sea drawn from the sand
> I grabbed the wife and kids and ran
> Please, God, save us! Please don't blame us,
> For this is the only life we have,
> We'll make it up if we were bad
> The wave was a'pounding
> We scrambled up the mountain
> No one even dared to turn their head
> Just one slip and you're dead. [71]

AN OTHER CUP

It is quite well recognized by the generation of that particular era, that one of my most influential and popular albums as Cat Stevens from the seventies was *Tea for the Tillerman*. You may have seen the record cover with a picture of a kind old red-bearded Tillerman drinking a cup of tea on a white-cloth table in the middle of the countryside, while a couple of boys are playing nearby, climbing the big tree under which he sits.

On *Tillerman* are some of my most famous songs like 'Father & Son', 'Wild World' and 'Where Do the Children Play?'. These have become reference points and the soundtrack to many people's lives. The album is considered a classic, probably because it captured the mood of the bedsitter crowd better than many others at the time. It made me into a household name all around the world, but especially in the US. My words of searching resonated in the hearts of the younger generation, who were also looking for alternatives to yesterday's world.

> Oh baby, baby it's a wild world
> It's hard to get by
> just upon a smile. [72]

In 2006 I released a new album called *An Other Cup*, after twenty-seven years of musical retreat. The title was a subtle reference to *Tea for the Tillerman*, indirectly I was saying: 'Well, if you liked the first cup, maybe you'll like another'. It certainly was a pleasant surprise to many ears, although criticisms came from some small sections of the Muslim community who had quite incredibly assumed that because I was making music I had left Islam – God forbid! The truth was that I had purposefully re-opened a bridge for me to cross and approach my friends and admirers of old, those whom I left stranded in 1979 and who had no other link to Islam except me and perhaps Muhammad Ali, the boxer – most other famous Muslims were politicians, tyrants or terrorists!

A brief look at the songs on my new album shows that my beliefs were well present in lyrics like 'Heaven/Where True Love Goes', and also in the song titles: 'Maybe There's A World' and 'The Beloved'. Most of my songs have a moral and ethical purpose without being preachy or too literal; that way people can discover for themselves the meanings of the songs and make their own private and personal voyage to the place I've been kindly permitted to show them.

> I dream of an open world, borderless and wide
> Where the people move from place to place,
> And nobody's taking sides
> Maybe there's a world that I'm still to find.
> Open up o world and let me in
> Then there'll be a new life to begin [73]

'Maybe There's A World' was actually one of the new songs from my musical in the making. I got together with a director from Sweden and we put on a few workshops in London with a handful of actors and singers. The script for the musical had made great advances and I was very excited by its adventurous theme and titled it *Moonshadow*!

'Criticisms came from some small sections of the Muslim community who had quite incredibly assumed that because I was making music I had left Islam – God forbid!'

Moonshadow was a brand new metaphorical adventure, a journey out of this world. The story begins on a faraway planet called *Alaylia*, a place of perpetual night where only a solitary Moon shines free. The poor worn-out people of this planet are forced to slave all their lives away working for the Zalim Empire and its ruler, Princess Zeena, just to earn enough to pay for light and heat. But there is a lively white-haired young boy called Stormy, who dreams of a beautiful bright world somewhere called *Shamsia*, where the Sun shines all day for free, nobody fights and people are kind and friendly to each other. One night he meets his Moonshadow who has been sent by a secret group of good shadows to help Stormy find this legendary dream world, and thus save the planet from Princess Zeena's sinister plan – to cause a total blackout through the death of the Moon.

Perhaps the plot sounds a bit fantastic? But the way the world is looking these days, for conscientious people and especially Muslims, the message is clear – or it should be.

> In this world of darkness
> Evil rules by night
> But somewhere in the shadows
> Someone's seeking light!
>
> No one loves their neighbours here
> Nobody has the time
> No one cares for anyone else
> In a world where the sun don't shine [74]

But the job of getting a musical on stage was a colossal one and needed a lot of money and extra support. There were still a lot of obstacles and it would take another few years before that happened.

Meantime, I wanted to get busy on a second album. I had just written an important milestone of a song called 'Roadsinger'. After *An Other Cup*, fans said they wanted to hear more of me with a guitar. So the next album was much more folk tale oriented. Apart from one track, all of it was recorded live. I listened to a lot of seventies L. A. music, such as Joni Mitchell, James Taylor, Carole King, and it inspired me to go back to that intimate style of recording. The songs are somewhat autobiographical but abstract enough so everyone can relate to them.

The album's title track was based on the story of a Roadsinger who is made an outcast by his old town. When he returns the people turn their backs, but a sweet young girl peeps out from behind a misty window and draws a message in the shape of a heart on the glass – there are definitely lots of symbolic meanings in that lyric.

But the question was: would the US authorities let me back in? Somehow the issue about me being on the No Fly List was quickly and sensibly resolved without much ado by simply following the advice of the US Consul General in Dubai. He suggested: 'Why don't you apply for a visa?' Well that sounded easy, and that is what I did. Lo and behold, the visa was granted. This time I got a very warm welcome when I arrived at Los Angeles airport and was met by a friendly Muslim police officer, who guided me swiftly through immigration.

Barack Obama had just been elected president and there seemed to be a wind of change in the air. The Bush legacy was rejected and Americans felt as if they wanted to come out of the cooler.

> Roadsinger came to town
> Long cape and hat
> People stood and stared
> Then closed their doors as he passed
> He strolled the empty street
> Kids banged on tin cans
> Then the panting dogs began to bark
> As the Roadsinger sang. [75]

MY PEOPLE

Before it all began I was actually moaning about the passing of the flowery sixties, where protests and the long marches for change swept the world. Then came the 'Arab Spring'.

How incredible that the new people's revolution was started (in a way) by a poor simple vegetable seller, Mohammed Bouazizi. This young man from Tunisia spent most of his days pushing a cart to sell his vegetables, but when town officials confiscated his cart, and his pleas for justice and mercy were ignored – something broke. A young man's fury against the system is now helping to transform the Middle East – but how will it end?

When people start to march, we see their hopes boldly displayed on banners and placards. Nobody could fail to be moved, as I was along with millions of others. I wrote a song with a simple chorus of two words: 'My People'. Then I got a lot of people from all round the world on Facebook to sing them with me. That was early on when the goal of the demonstrations were manifestly clear and straightforward: to be rid of entrenched tyrants.

I recorded the song in Berlin 100 yards from where the East–West wall fell.

> 'Next to Prayer comes Charity; paying the poor due to those in need. Remember also that the Arab awakening began with a poor vegetable-seller!'

My People
When you gonna leave my People?
Give them room to breathe
My People
Stop oppressing
My People
All they want is bread and clothes
Space to rest and left alone
My People
When you gonna free my People?
Let them live in peace
My People [76]

As time passed we saw the signs of frustration. Naturally, people wanted change quickly and were losing patience, as the Almighty says: 'Man was ever hasty.'[77] Some have waited forty years and are willing to wait a few years longer, but many want it now.

The slogan 'No More!' united the hearts of young and old, rich and poor, male and female. But as the dust settled, it seemed the divisions that bedevilled the Muslim lands were returning and only getting deeper. The time period required to really make a lasting change had to be longer than just a quick rush to have elections. Now we were witnessing the gap widen between the new 'revolutionaries' and the old revolutionaries under a new name: 'the elected Government', while the military stood by to oversee the whole drama, pulling the rug from under the feet of anyone they considered unworthy or who had overstayed their democratically appointed seat.

But somehow, somewhere between the massive cogwheels of governmental bureaucracy, a screw has fallen out. Change has to start with looking after the weaker elements of society, that was always the structure and principle in the Prophet's teachings: Next to Prayer (*Salat*) comes Charity (*Zakat*); paying the poor due to those in need. Remember also that the Arab awakening began with a poor vegetable-seller!

Looking back at the sixties, as now, the leadership even then seemed disunited. There were slogans, icons and anthems; the dawn of the new age never came, but the riot police did, along with commercialization and the return of 'business as usual'. Will barbed wire be rolled out again? Will we see more tanks? Will the high walls of the political elite be rebuilt, even higher?

The longer you live (or the more you take history seriously) the more you realize the repetitious nature of life is exactly that: it repeats itself. In musical terms it's like a chorus, here it comes again, 'Oh baby, baby it's a Wild World!' Remember that one?

In scientific terms the splitting up and separation of things is a universal phenomenon and occurrence, it is the basis of Chaos theory; in political terms – the way things look in some Muslim countries – you might call this fragmentation a civil war, or (as some call it) induced 'democracy'. What we are witnessing is nothing new. If we take a really long leap back in religious terms we can see that the universe began with the heavens and the earth being joined, and then – they separated.

Mankind also began as one unit of man and wife, and it is a fact that human beings inevitably differ and split with one another, except those whom Allah guides; this is mentioned in the Qur'an:

> **Mankind was one community, and Allah sent (unto them) prophets as bearers of good tidings and as warners, and revealed therewith the Scripture with the truth that it might judge between mankind concerning that wherein they differed. And only those unto whom (the Scripture) was given differed concerning it, after clear proofs had come unto them, through hatred one of another. And Allah by His Will guided those who believe unto the truth of that concerning which they differed. Allah guides whom He wills unto a straight path.** [78]

The point I am trying to make is that, even though there is natural diversity in the Almighty's creation, with humankind branching into various beautiful races, languages and colours, this is actually a blessing and should encourage us to know and respect each other better.[79] This does not separate us from our common bond in the noble house of humanity. Yet divisions based on pride, allegiance and self-interest often appear and then break us up further, leading to conflicts under the influence of the whispering Satan.

But there is a way of mending things and building human unity – through effort by following the guidance of Allah. Adam, the forefather of mankind, repented after he and Eve ate from the forbidden tree, then they were given 'Words of Guidance'. That's when the work started.

> **We said: Go down, all of you, from hence; but verily there comes unto you from Me a guidance; then whoso follows My guidance, there shall no fear come upon them neither shall they grieve.** [80]

'The longer you live (or the more you take history seriously) the more you realize the repetitious nature of life is exactly that: it repeats itself.'

The way to peace and bridging divisions is again, through hard work. And that comes back to *Da'wah*. According to the great scholar, Imam Shafi', the following short chapter called *Time* would have been enough to guide the believers, even if no other verse or chapter of the Qur'an had been revealed.

> By [the passing of] Time
> Verily mankind is in loss
> Except such as believe and do good works, and enjoin on one another Truth, and enjoin on one another, patience. [81]

The Prophet (peace be upon him) warned us also about partisanship, the greatest destructive curse on the world today, and he enjoined us to avoid backbiting, hurting others and especially *fitnah* (trials, conflicts and discord), which Allah says in the Qur'an is worse than slaughter.[82] It is easy to get angry at the state of the world and that's when certain voices get louder and may pressurize us. But we should beware of falling into more evil.

One of the companions, Hudhaifa B. Al Yaman, asked the Messenger of God regarding the future of Muslims, and how to respond in certain evil circumstances:

> 'O Allah's apostle! We were in ignorance and in evil and Allah has bestowed upon us the present good; will there be any evil after this good?' The Prophet replied, 'Yes.' I asked, 'Will there be good after that evil?' He said, 'Yes, but it would be tainted with Dakhan (i.e. little evil).' I asked, 'What will its Dakhan be?' He said, 'There will be some people who will lead (people) according to principles other than my tradition. You will see their actions and disapprove of them.' I said, 'Will there be any evil after that good?' He said, 'Yes, there will be some people who will invite others to the doors of Hell, and whoever accepts their invitation to it will be thrown in it (by them).' I said, 'O Allah's apostle! Describe those people to us.' He said, 'They will belong to us and speak our language' I asked, 'What do you order me to do if such a thing should take place in my life?' He said, 'adhere to the wide-group of Muslims and their Imam.' I asked, 'If there is neither a wide-group (of Muslims) nor an Imam (what shall I do)?' He said, 'Keep away from all those different sects, even if you had to bite (i.e. eat) the root of a tree, till you meet Allah while you are still in that state.'[83]

We must beware of ignorance and anarchy, two great evils. The Prophet warned us about the evil that overtakes people if they follow the wrong type of people or leadership. The *fitnah*[84] that results is visible today, but some have not yet learned.

We can only succeed if we stick to the path laid out by the last Messenger of God (peace be upon him) and if the Almighty gives us *tawfiq* (ability) to do so.

He taught the people to worship
Bowing to one God, bowing to one God
His mercy stretched from east to West
To every man woman and child
He was born to be the Beloved
A Will of the Divine
He was born to be the Beloved
Nature Sublime. [85]

GOD IS THE LIGHT

On the Day of Judgement we will all have our records open and everything we have done will be exposed. That is the Day we will all know the truth or error of our ways. Only the mercy of Allah can save us from perdition and punishment.

What I have written here might upset some people or cause a bit of disruption to their perceptions, but I sincerely hope that it will enlighten and put the majority of hearts to rest, removing those doubts which may have been raised about me, as well as my work and intentions.

It must be clearly stated here that a person does not leave Islam because he or she does not subscribe to or follow a certain view or *fatwah*, particularly when there are justifiable and opposing points of view based on numerous pieces of evidence. People who rush to judge others simply because of a difference in *fiqh* (understanding) are more in danger than anyone to fall into error and should remember the dangers to themselves.

The following verse was revealed regarding the Prophet David after Allah had tested him; having heard the argument of two contending brothers it seems David judged too soon, and Allah knows best.

> O David, indeed We have made you a successor upon the earth, so judge between the people in truth and do not follow [your own] desire, as it will lead you astray from the way of Allah. Indeed, those who go astray from the way of Allah will have a severe punishment for having forgotten the Day of Account. [86]

I have tried to follow the Prophet's advice (as quoted in the beginning of this book) by speaking out and not allowing Satan to dictate or rule the agenda by trying to explain things better and more clearly and not hiding the truth. We must realize that the only real conspiracy theory to believe is the one regarding Satan himself, and that's not a theory – it's a fact – he is actually the evil mastermind behind the worst things that are happening in the world. The only help we have against him is the guidance and support of Allah, the Sustainer of the heavens and the earth.

In an increasingly secularized world, the greatest service we can do is to worship Allah purely, and study His words; to understand – as far as we are able – what Allah expects from us in every given situation. The Prophet (peace be upon him) – the last of the prophets was sent as a guide for all time, until the Last Day. If we continue to pray and give in charity and remind each other of the truth and have patience, maybe we will be forgiven all the things we did and said that were wrong.

I am not seeking or asking anyone to follow me, or my various conclusions, but only to look within themselves at the signs of the eternal truth which have already been placed there by the Creator. The Prophet (peace be upon him), continuously urged the Companions to seek the help and guidance of Allah in all matters where there is a choice.[87]

In the end, I sincerely pray that Allah will overlook whatever faults I may have committed in trying to fulfil my promise and in my zeal to help further the teaching and understanding of Islam, to spread the word of peace and encourage unity – even if sometimes I spoke or sung out of tune.

> 'People who rush to judge others simply because of a difference in *fiqh* (understanding) are more in danger than anyone to fall into error and should remember the dangers to themselves.'

The Prophet (peace be upon him), is reported in a *Hadith Qudsi*[88] to have said the following:

> Allah, Blessed and Exalted is He, says, 'O son of Adam, as long as you call on Me, I shall forgive you of what you have done, and think nothing of it. O son of Adam, even if your sins were to reach up to the clouds in the sky, and then you were to ask for My forgiveness, I would forgive you and think nothing of it. O son of Adam, even if you were to come to Me with sins nearly as great as the earth, and then you were to meet Me after death, not worshipping anything besides Me, I would bring you forgiveness nearly as great as it.'[89]

As Cat Stevens' or now as Yusuf Islam, I have been put in a unique position where I have become a looking glass, through which the West can see Islam, and Muslims can see the West. The possibility that my abstinence and withdrawal from music might lead people away from knowing a straight path to Paradise or into thinking that Islam was too narrow, not relevant to them and had little to offer the world in terms of culture, art and aesthetics, seriously disturbed me. Equally, I was also concerned that Muslims might prejudge my actions or interpret them negatively without at least trying to understand my Islamic reasoning. Although I do recognize the dangers of music becoming a catchy trend rather than a God-conscious and ethical pastime or work, I believe it is up to every individual to guard themselves against misguidance. Blocking the road to what is allowed is not the way of Islam or the blessed Prophet (peace be upon him), he always made it easy for people.

My real objective in making my life and views public is to encourage everybody (Muslims as well as non-Muslims) to study Islam for themselves, as I did, and explore what Allah the Most Merciful and Majestic has revealed through His beloved Messenger (peace be upon him) as mercy and guidance for all humanity.

> **Say, 'O mankind, the truth has come to you from your Lord, so whoever is guided is only guided for [the benefit of] his soul, and whoever goes astray only goes astray [in violation] against it. And I am not a warder over you.'** [90]

ENDNOTES

1. *Sahih Al Bukhari*, vol.3, book 33, chapter 11, Hadith 2038
2. The collected reports and quotes of the Prophet memorized and written during his life
3. A separate, more comprehensive booklet on the subject has been written, entitled 'Fatwahs and Opinions on Music and Other Issues'
4. The Qur'an, Surat Al Anbiya, (The Prophets), 21:25
5. Abdullah bin 'Amr narrated that Allah's Messenger (may peace be upon him) said: 'The Antichrist would appear in my Ummah and he would stay (in the world) for forty – "I cannot say whether he meant forty days, forty months or forty years" – and Allah would then send Jesus son of Mary who would resemble Urwa b Mas'ud. He (Jesus Christ) would chase him and kill him. Then people would live for seven years that there would be no rancour between two persons.' (*Sahih Muslim*, book 041, *Hadith* 7023)
6. *Sahih Al Bukhari*, vol.1, book 3, chapter 11, *Hadith* 69
7. There Is No God But Allah
8. The Qur'an, Surat Al Inshiqaq, (The Sundering), 84:19
9. The period of ignorance before Islam
10. Cat Stevens, 'The Road to Findout', *Tea for the Tillerman* (Island Records, 1970)
11. Cat Stevens, 'I Wish, I Wish', *Mona Bone Jakon*, (Island Records, 1970)
12. Cat Stevens, 'Miles From Nowhere', *Tea for the Tillerman* (Island Records, 1970)
13. Cat Stevens, 'The Wind', *Teaser and the Firecat* (Island Records, 1971)
14. The Qur'an, Surat Al 'Alaq, (The Blood Clot), 96: 1- 5
15. The Qur'an, Surat Al Fatihah, (The Opening), 1:1-2
16. The Qur'an, Surat Ash Shura, The Council, 42:13
17. The Qur'an, Surat Al Anbiya, (The Prophets), 21:30
18. The Qur'an, Surat Al An'am, (The Cattle), 6:125
19. The Testimony of Faith ('There is No God But Allah')
20. Cat Stevens, 'Daytime', *Back to Earth* (Island Records, 1978)

21 Permissible, allowed
22 Amazingly, by the Grace of Allah, Peter became Sulaiman, a Muslim. He married a Somali lady who bore him two daughters.
23 Cat Stevens, 'Father & Son', *Tea for the Tillerman* (Island Records, 1970)
24 The call to Prayer made five times a day from minarets and mosques around the world
25 Authenticated and approved sayings, actions and approvals of the Prophet Muhammad (peace be upon him)
26 Cat Stevens, 'Sitting', *Catch Bull At Four* (Island Records, 1972)
27 The word, *salafa* means that which is past; used to refer to the early period of the Pious Predecessors in Islamic history
28 *Maliki, Shafi'i, Hanafi* and *Hanbali* (schools within Sunni Islam)
29 *Ja'fari* (a school within Shia Islam)
30 The Qur'an, Surat Al Imran, (The Family of 'Imran), 3:31
31 Successorship to the Prophet (peace be upon him)
32 The Qur'an, Surat An Nisa, (Women), 4:59
33 The Qur'an, Surat Al Hujurat (The Private Apartments), 49:9
34 Leviticus, 24: 16, 'Anyone who blasphemes the name of the Lord is to be put to death. The entire assembly must stone them. Whether foreigner or native-born, when they blaspheme the Name they are to be put to death.'
35 The press release released in March 1989 stated, 'Under the Islamic law, Muslims are bound to keep within the limits of the law of the country in which they live, providing that it does not restrict the freedom to worship and serve God and fulfil their basic religious duties (*Fard 'Ayn*)...If we can't get satisfaction within the present limits of the law, like a ban on this blasphemous book, *Satanic Verses* which insults God and His Prophets – including those Prophets honoured by Christians, Jews as well as Muslims – this does not mean that we should step outside of the law to find redress, no.'
36 Most of the Muslim participants of the programme – including myself – complained to the British Independent Television Network about the brutal editing of the discussions. However, one positive comment was included: the last and ultimate question posed on the TV debate was when the QC asked me to consider the scenario whereby I was the foreman of the Jury at the Old Bailey court, 'If Salman Rushdie was taken to the Old Bailey court and the Jury voted 10 to 2, to acquit (Rushdie) … what would you say as foreman of the Jury?' 'Not guilty,' I stated. It was the final word of the programme. For further insights listen to 'Editing Floor Blues', *Tell 'Em I'm Gone* (Sony Records, 2014)
37 *Sahih Al Bukhari*, vol. 4, book 60, chapter 50, *Hadith* 3461
38 A verse of the Qur'an revealed after the Prophet's migration to Madinah where the injunctions of society were further detailed and defined, and war in the cause of defence of Islam was permitted.
39 The Qur'an, Surat An Nahl, (The Bee), 16:90
40 *Sahih Al Bukhari*, vol. 9, book 92, chapter 5, *Hadith* 7062/63
41 The Qur'an, Surat An Nisa, (Women), 4:94
42 The words of the song reportedly sung by children and well-wishers on the arrival of the Prophet to Madinah
43 Cat Stevens, 'Peace Train', *Teaser and the Firecat* (Island Records, 1971)
44 *Sahih Muslim*
45 *Istihsan* (seeking what is good or better)

46 Shama'il Tirmidhi, 235: 5
47 The inference of Law through 'independent reasoning'; making effort to come to a judgement in conformity with Islam where no clear ruling is found in the Qur'an or Sunnah
48 The Ottoman *Khilafa* developed the *Millet* system, offering separate legal courts for Christians, Jews and communities to rule themselves.
49 Cat Stevens 'O Very Young', *Buddha & the Chocolate Box* (Island Records, 1974)
50 The Qur'an, (The Tablespread), 5:32
51 Yusuf Islam, 'God is the Light', *Footsteps in the Light* (Jamal Records, 2006)
52 *Sahih Al Bukhari*, vol. 2, book 13, chapter 3, *Hadith* 952
53 Ibn Hajar, Fathul-Bari, Fiqh-us-Sunnah vol.2, Fiqh 2.153
54 Yusuf Islam, *A is for Allah* (Mountain of Light, 2000)
55 Yusuf Islam 'The Little Ones (of Sarajevo and Dunblane)', *I Have No Cannons That Roar* (Jamal Records, 2000)
56 Dr Irfan Ljubijankić, 'I Have No Cannons That Roar' performed by Dino Merlin (Jamal Records, 2000)
57 A tambourine without bells
58 Yusuf Islam, *I Look I See* (Jamal Records, 2003)
59 The Qur'an, Surat Al A'raf, (The Heights), 7:32-33
60 The Principles of Jurisprudence
61 The Qur'an, Surat Al Anfal, (Spoils of War), 8:20-21
62 The Qur'an, Surat Luqman, (Luqman), 31:6
63 In *Sahih Al Bukhari* it is reported: 'Aishah narrated that when a woman was married to an Ansari man, the Prophet (peace be upon him) said, "Aishah, did they have any entertainment (*Lahw*)? The Ansar are fond of entertainment."'
64 The Qur'an, Surat Al Isra, (The Night Journey), 17:64
65 'Narrated Abu Amir or Abu Malik Al Ashari that he heard the Prophet saying, "From among my followers there will be some people who will consider illegal sexual intercourse, the wearing of silk, the drinking of alcoholic drinks and the use of musical instruments, as lawful. And there will be some people who will stay near the side of a mountain and in the evening their shepherd will come to them with their sheep and ask them for something, but they will say to him, 'Return to us tomorrow.' Allah will destroy them during the night and will let the mountain fall on them, and He will transform the rest of them into monkeys and pigs and they will remain so till the Day of Resurrection."' Sahih Al Bukhari, vol. 7, book 74, chapter 6, *Hadith* 5590
66 It is to be noted that the *Hadith in Sahih Al Bukhari* specifically refers to silk as being made *Halal* by certain sinful members of the Muslim *Ummah* (implying that silk – along with alcohol, illegal sexual intercourse and musical instruments – were all ostensibly and indisputably known to be *Haram*). While it is a well-known fact that silk is *Halal* for ladies; it is also allowed to make and trade silk shirts or garments for men as well as ladies; it's allowed for males to wear it in limited measure; and if a person has a skin ailment it is allowed for him/her to wear silk. Therefore silk is not entirely *Haram* and its prohibition conditional and limited. Remember, this in addition to the fact that the *Hadith* mentioned is already disputed and considered by some scholars as unconfirmed because of a break in its chain of authority before it reached Imam Bukhari.
67 Such as the *Hadith* related by Ibn Majah: 'The Messenger (pbuh) of Allah (SWT) said, "Some people of my *Ummah* will drink wine, calling it by other than its real

name, merriment will be made for them through the playing of musical instruments and the singing of lady singers. Allah will cleave the earth under them and turn others into monkeys and swine.'" This *Hadith* does not mention the people considering what is *haram* to be *halal*, except in the case of wine. The music and singing girls are simply an accompaniment. This does not clearly state or imply all singing and music on other lawful occasions are prohibited.

68   The Qur'an, Surat An Nisa, (Women), 4:31
69   Again it is interesting to note that in one famous collection of 'Major Sins' by Shams Al Deen Dhahabi, music is not mentioned at all; yet drawing figures, gambling, disobedience to parents, dragging one's garment out of pride, arguing, picking apart another's words and quarrelling and many others are.
70   Yusuf, 'Boots and Sand', *Roadsinger* (Island Records, 2009)
71   Yusuf Islam, 'Indian Ocean', *Gold* (Universal Records, 2005)
72   Cat Stevens, 'Wild World', *Tea for the Tillerman* (Island Records, 1970)
73   Yusuf, 'Maybe There's A World', *An Other Cup* (Polydor Records, London, 2006; Atlantic Records, USA, 2006)
74   Yusuf, 'World of Darkness', *Roadsinger* (Island Records, 2009)
75   Yusuf, 'Roadsinger', *Roadsinger* (Island Records, 2009)
76   www.yusufislam.com
77   The Qur'an, Surat Al Isra, (The Night Journey), 17:11
78   The Qur'an, Surat Al Baqarah, (The Cow), 2:213
79   'And among His Signs is the creation of the heavens and the earth, and the difference of your languages and colours. Verily, in that are indeed signs for those of sound knowledge.' (The Qur'an, Surat Ar-Rum, (The Romans), 30:22). And also: 'O mankind! We have created you from a male and a female, and made you into nations and tribes, that you may know one another.' (The Qur'an, Surat Al Hujarat, (The Private Apartments), 49:13).
80   The Qur'an, Surat Al Baqarah, (The Cow), 2:38
81   The Qur'an, Surat Al 'Asr, (Time), 103:1-3
82   The Qur'an, Surat Al Baqarah, (The Cow), 2:191
83   *Sahih Al Bukhari*, vol.4, Book 56, Hadith 803
84   Trials, conflict, discord
85   Yusuf, 'The Beloved', *An Other Cup* (Polydor Records, London; Atlantic Records, 2006)
86   The Qur'an, Surat Sad, 38:26
87   The Prophet taught his companions *Du'ah Istikharah* (a prayer for guidance): 'Oh Allah, I seek your counsel by your knowledge and I seek your assistance by your power and I ask You from your immense favour, for verily You are able while I am not, and verily You know while I do not, and You are the knower of the unseen. O Allah, if You know this affair (*mention the matter here*) to be good for me in relation to my religion, my life and aftermath, my present and future, then decree it and facilitate it for me, and bless me with it, and if You know this affair to be ill for me concerning my religion, my life and end, my present and future, then remove it from me and remove me from it, and decree for me what is good, whatever it may be, and make me satisfied with it.'
88   A Holy Saying of God
89   *Hadith* al Qudsi reported by At Tirmidhi
90   The Qur'an, Surat Yunus (Jonah), 10:108

IMAGE CREDITS

Reasons: Bastakiya, Dubai; 2006; Peter Sanders. **Background:** circa 1965; Getty Images. **The Qur'an:** Dome of the Rock, Jerusalem; Faris Baidoun; Shutterstock. **Shahadah:** 1973; Chris Walter; Getty Images. **The Community:** circa 1981; DMG Media. **The Muslim World:** Sudan; Peter Sanders. **Trouble:** The ruins of a family home, Kosovo; 1998; courtesy Yusuf Islam. **The Call:** California; Jesse Dylan. **Da'wah:** The Market Hall Theatre, Johannesburg; 2003; courtesy Yusuf Islam. **Children and Song:** A is for Allah; 2000; courtesy Yusuf Islam. **A Guitar Comes Home:** Market Coffee House, London; Muhammad Yusuf. **The New Wave:** Malibu beach; Jim McCrary; Getty Images. **An Other Cup:** Bastakiya, Dubai; 2006; Peter Sanders. **My People:** The Mawazine Festival, Rabat, Morocco; Aminah Yusuf. **God is the Light:** Sheikh Zayed Grand Mosque, Abu Dhabi, UAE; Patryk Kosmider; Shutterstock.

KEY TERMS

Adhan: Islam's call to Prayer.

Allah Karim: God is most Kind and Generous.

Ansar: The citizens of Madinah who helped the Prophet Muhammad after he left Makkah.

Aqidah: The foundations of faith; any religious belief system or creed.

As-salamu alaykum: The Muslim greeting meaning 'may peace be upon you'.

Ayatollah: A religious leader among Shi'ah Muslims; a high-ranking religious authority regarded by his followers as the most learned person of his age.

Bismillah: The short term of the full phrase *Bismillah ir-Rahman ir-Rahim*; meaning 'In the name of Allah the Mercifeul, the Most Kind.'

Bu-ath: A location close to Madinah where a fierce battle took place between the tribes before the Prophet Muhammad's arrival.

Caliph: A title for the religious and civil rulers of the Islamic world claiming succession from Prophet Muhammad.

Da'wah: Conveying the message of Islam; calling people to God

'Eid: Two major religious holidays celebrated by Muslims worldwide, marking the end of Ramadan and the completion of Pilgramage, *Hajj*.

Fatwah: A legal opinion or learned interpretation issued by Muslim jurists on any matter not already clearly defined by the Qur'an or the sayings of the Prophet.

Fitnah: An Arabic word with extensive connotations of trial, affliction or distress.

Fiqh: Islamic jurisprudence and legal opinions dealing with the observance of rituals, morals and social legislation in Islam.

Hadith: The recorded reports of the Prophet's sayings, actions and approvals.

Halal: Any object or an action which is permissible to use or engage in.

Haram: Used to refer to any act forbidden by Allah.

Ijma: A consensus of the Muslim learned regarding religious issues.

Ijtihad: Independent reasoning based on the Qur'an and Sunnah.

Imam: An Islamic leader; someone who leads Islamic worship services and provides religious guidance to the community.

Istihsan: A juristic preference which Muslim scholars may use to express their preference for a particular judgment in Islamic law over alternatives.

Jahiliyyah: An Islamic concept of the ignorance of divine guidance or a state of ignorance of guidance from God.

Jihad: A struggle for God's cause. A wide interpretation can include internal or exteral effort in eradicating injustice and applying God's commands on an individual or collective level.

Lahw: Forms of entertainment: a pastime, activity or diversion.

La ilaha illa-Allah (Shahadah): There is no god but the God (Allah).

Madhhab: Pathway of Islamic understanding; a school of thought in jurisprudence.

Madinah: A holy city in Islam, second only to Makkah. Madinah is the burial place of the Prophet Muhammad.

Makkah: Often known as Mecca. A sacred place where Muslims go to perform pilgrimage (Hajj) and Umrah.

Makruh: A disliked or offensive act; such acts are not absolutely forbidden, but a person who abstains from them will be rewarded.

Ma'ruf: A meaning that is commonly known, understood, recognized, acknowledged and accepted.

Masalas: Questions with juristic answers.

Munqati: A *hadith* described this way is one in which the chain of people reporting the hadith is disconnected at any point.

Nasheeds: Islamic vocal music that is usually sung a cappella or accompanied by percussion instruments such as a duff.

Qur'an: The religious text of Islam, revealed by God to the Last Prophet, Muhammad, through Angel Gabriel.

Sahabah: The companions of the Prophet Muhammad.

Sahih Bukhari: One of the six major *Hadith* collections of Sunni Islam.

Salafi: A movement based on the way of the pious predecessors; the name refers to the earliest Muslims who its adherents believe provide the epitome of Islamic practice.

Salam: Peace and security.

Salat: The practice of ritualistic prayer in Islam as opposed to *dua*. Its importance for Muslims is indicated by its status as one of the Five Pillars of Islam.

Sheikh: A term of respect in the Arabic language that literally means elder. It is commonly used to designate the elder of a tribe, a revered wise man, or an Islamic scholar.

Shari'ah: The moral code and religious law of a prophetic religion.

Shaytan: Satan.

Shi'ah: The followers of Muhammad's son-in-law and cousin Ali, whom the Shi'ah believe to be Muhammad's successor in the Caliphate. They represent the second largest denomination of Muslims.

Sufism: A term belonging to different orders or congregations, usually connected to a Sheikh or spiritual teacher.

Sunnah: The way of life prescribed as normative for Muslims on the basis of the teachings and practices of Prophet Muhammad.

Sunni: The largest branch of Islam, its adherents are referred to as people of the tradition of Muhammad and the consensus of the Ummah.

Tabligh: Conveying Islam.

Tablighi Jamat: An Islamic movement reaching out to Muslims across social and economic spectra to bring them in line with the group's understanding of Islam.

Tafsir: The explanation or interpretation of text in the Qur'an.

Taif: A city in the Makkah province of Saudi Arabia.

Taqleed: To follow someone, to imitate; to follow an interpreter of religious law.

Tawfiq: Good fortune, success and God-given ability.

Thawb: An ankle-length garment worn by men in Arab countries.

Ummah: A nation or community; in the Qur'an it is referred to as a single group that shares common beliefs, specifically those that are the objects of a divine plan of salvation.

'Umrah: A pilgrimage to Makkah performed by Muslims, undertaken at any time of the year.

'Urf: The traditions and customs of people.

'Usul al Fiqh: The study of the origins, sources, and principles upon which Islamic jurisprudence is based.